Epiphany

Aids for Interpreting
the Lessons of the Church Year

Epiphany

Marianne H. Micks

Elizabeth Achtemeier, series editor

Series A

FORTRESS PRESS   Philadelphia

Library of Congress Cataloging in Publication Data

Main entry under title:

Proclamation 3.

Consists of 28 volumes in 3 series designated A, B, and C which correspond to the cycles of the three year lectionary. Each series contains 8 basic volumes with the following titles: Advent-Christmas, Epiphany, Lent, Holy Week, Easter, Pentecost 1, Pentecost 2, and Pentecost 3.
1. Bible—Homiletical use. 2. Bible—Liturgical lessons, English. I. Achtemeier, Elizabeth Rice, 1926–   .
BS534.5.P765   1985   251   84–18756
ISBN 0–8006–4106–X (Series B, Pentecost 1)

2551A86   Printed in the United States of America   1–4118

Contents

Series Foreword

Proclamation 3 is an entirely new aid for preaching from the three-year ecumenical lectionary. In outward appearance this new series is similar to *Proclamation: Aids for Interpreting the Lessons of the Church Year* and *Proclamation 2*. But *Proclamation 3* has a new content as well as a new purpose.

First, there is only one author for each of the twenty-eight volumes of *Proclamation 3*. This means that each author handles both the exegesis and the exposition of the stated texts, thus eliminating the possibility of disparity between scholarly apprehension and homiletical application of the appointed lessons. While every effort was made in *Proclamation: Aids* and in *Proclamation 2* to avoid such disparity, it tended to creep in occasionally. *Proclamation 3* corrects that tendency.

Second, *Proclamation 3* is directed primarily at homiletical interpretation of the stated lessons. We have again assembled the finest biblical scholars and preachers available to write for the series; now, however, they bring their skills to us not primarily as exegetes, but as interpreters of the Word of God. Exegetical material is still presented—sometimes at length—but, most important, here it is also applied; the texts are interpreted and expounded homiletically for the church and society of our day. In this new series scholars become preachers. They no longer stand back from the biblical text and just discuss it objectively. The engage it—as the Word of God for the worshiping community. The reader therefore will not find here the divisions between "exegesis" and "homiletical interpretation" that were marked off in the two earlier series. In *Proclamation 3* the work of the pulpit is the context and goal of all that is written.

There is still some slight diversity between the several lections and calendars of the various denominations. In an effort to overcome such diversity, the North American Committee on a Common Lectionary issued an experimental "consensus lectionary" *(The Common Lectionary),* which is now being tried out in some congregations and which will be further altered at the end of a three-year period. When the final form of that lectionary appears, *Proclamation* will take account of it. In the meantime, *Proclamation 3* deals with those texts that are used by *most* denominations on any given Sunday. It also continues to use the Lutheran numbering of the Sundays "after Pentecost." But Episcopalians and Roman Catholics will find most of their stated propers dealt with under this numbering.

Each author writes on three lessons for each Sunday, but no one method of combining the appointed lessons has been imposed upon the writers. The texts are sometimes treated separately, sometimes together—according to the author's own understanding of the texts' relationships and messages. The authors interpret the appointed texts as these texts have spoken to them.

Dr. Marianne Micks is Professor of Biblical and Historical Theology at the Protestant Episcopal Theological Seminary in Alexandria, Va. Holding a doctorate from Yale University, she has served as a campus minister for the Episcopal Church at Smith College and at the University of California at Berkeley. She was chairman of the Department of Religion at Western College for four years and subsequently Dean of the College. She has written six books, including *The Joy of Worship* and *Our Search for Identity*.

The Epiphany of Our Lord

Lutheran	Roman Catholic	Episcopal	Pres/UCC/Chr	Meth/COCU
Isa. 60:1–6	Isa. 60:1–6	Isa. 60:1–6, 9	Isa. 60:1–8	Isa. 60:1–6
Eph. 3:2–12	Eph. 3:2–3, 5–6	Eph. 3:1–12	Eph. 3:1–6	Eph. 3:1–12
Matt. 2:1–12	Matt. 2:1–12	Matt. 2:1–12	Matt. 2:1–12	Matt. 2:1–12

The three readings for the Epiphany proclaim one common message: The saving work of God is for all people everywhere. Thus they announce the central theme of this whole season of the church year, that of God's shining forth among all nations. It is the season for affirming what God has done and is doing among us. It is a season for breaking down walls of separation and for building up discipleship.

The poetry of the Old Testament lesson pictures gift-laden caravans from the East streaming toward a Jerusalem bright with the glory of God. The epistle underlines the great Pauline insight that all people share in Christ Jesus, whatever their ethnic background. And the gemlike tale of the Magi from Matthew's Gospel repeats the good news in narrative form. In it both nature and Scripture point to the one who unites the great and the small, the near and the far.

FIRST LESSON: ISAIAH 60:1–6

This is part of a longer, unified poem usually attributed to the anonymous postexilic prophet sometimes called "Third Isaiah." The author is clearly a disciple of his predecessor, "Second Isaiah," but writing for a new situation, probably around 538 B.C., after some exiles have returned to the city but before life has become much better than it was in captivity in Babylon. To a city gray with gloom the poet addresses the ringing imperatives: Rise! Shine!

Rise? The image is one of a woman flat on her face in the dust. Perhaps we need to transpose the image into a person slumped in a chair in front of the TV, so dejected as to be without spark of hope or purpose. To such a person, to such people, the poet says not only, "Get up!" He adds, "Shine!"

Claus Westermann believes that the writer has in mind "a beaming look on the face." But that does not mean simply a fatuous smile akin to one of those orange stickers of a round face with up-curved mouth. Echoes of other encounters with the glory of the Lord are many. A major allusion is to Moses' shining countenance after he spoke with God atop Mount Sinai (Exod. 33:11), a bit of Israel's memory reinterpreted by Paul in 2 Cor. 3:7. In its original context the image suggests that this is the way any person looks to whom the Lord speaks "face to face, as a man speaks to his friend" (Exod. 33:11). The same idea is expressed here in v. 5. When you see what good things the Lord is doing, you shall "be radiant." Indeed you will be bursting with joy.

Notice the movement in this poem. Because of its long association with the Gospel story of the Magi we usually think of kings coming from the East. But the poet wants us to picture a great homecoming in Jerusalem. The first stress is on the return of sons and daughters, walking home, even being carried home. It is a return of exiles to their native city. They are followed by riches pouring into the city from both east and west. The "abundance of the sea" does not mean just fish. In parallel with "the wealth of nations," it means all that can be carried by great ships on the Mediterranean, as well as all that can be carried by camel trains from such trade centers as Sheba in Arabia. Some listeners will be reminded of the visit of the Queen of Sheba to King Solomon. She came with "a very great retinue" of camels bearing spices, gold, and precious stones (1 Kings 10:2).

All of this wealth and all of these peoples who bring it are "to proclaim the praise of the Lord." It is the Lord who has ushered in this bright new day. Ultimately it is the Lord who has returned to Jerusalem. This personal meaning of the word "glory" is well conveyed by the translation that renders *kabod* simply as Presence (JPS). This Presence is key to the rejoicing the poet calls for.

SECOND LESSON: EPHESIANS 3:2–12

Read in juxtaposition to the Isaiah passage, this section of Ephesians presents a striking twist of theme. Whereas there we saw the wealth of nations flowing into Jerusalem, now we hear of boundless wealth flowing from Jerusalem, as it were, to all nations. That is the impact of the Pauline metaphor, "the unsearchable riches of Christ" (v. 8), now being proclaimed to the whole human race.

A preacher could preach for a lifetime from this pericope without

exhausting its riches. It is a tightly packed précis of Pauline theology
—an example of why some scholars say that Ephesians is more
Pauline than Paul. One could use this passage for a book on key
Pauline terms such as grace, gospel, faith, church.

In the Epiphany setting, however, the emphasis should be on the
twice-repeated *now* (vv. 5, 10). Something new has happened. Something new is now being shown forth. Something new has been un-
veiled for all to see. Although it is part of God's eternal plan and
purpose, it is only now that we human beings are empowered to see
the plan, to hear the good news: we all have access to our Lord.

The text poses several problems for today's interpreter. First the
meaning of the recurring word *mystery* needs to be clarified. Contemporary theologians often insist on a notion of Mystery that is part of
God's very being and part of any experience of transcendence. In this
sense Mystery is to be affirmed with awe, not cleared up like the
"mystery" of a detective story with no puzzlement left over. Yet in
this passage *mystery* is precisely that which has been and is being
revealed through the power of the Spirit.

A second problem, and a real one for many whose ears are sensitive
to inclusive language today, is the idiom "the sons of men" (v. 5). It is
noteworthy that the NEB renders the sense of the idiom accurately as
"the human race." This is surely consonant with the inclusive understanding of the gift of Christ in the passage as a whole.

Third, one must wrestle with the difficult thought of v. 10. In
Pauline understanding "the principalities and powers in heavenly
places" refer to superhuman beings which were created by God but
which misused their freedom and hence became agents of evil. Now in
Christ they have been conquered (cf. Rom. 8:38–39). Yet here the
author asserts that the church has a part in making known to them the
wonderful Wisdom of God. The thought is closely related to that of
Col. 1:15–20 where the cosmic scope of Christ's reconciling work is
proclaimed, as well as Christ's headship over his body, the church. In
both cases the subject is what Augustine called "the whole Christ,"
head and members.

Whatever difficulties one encounters in the details of the text,
however, the unifying message is unambiguous. In Christ, God has
now made known his universal plan for the whole human family. He is
the light to all the nations.

Gentile ears have so long heard and accepted the good news of our inclusion in the plan of salvation that it is almost impossible for us to recapture any sense of surprise about the fact. For Paul it was, of course, an earthshaking, soul-shattering revelation. The preacher focusing on this text needs to find some way to express the shock value of the triple claim made in v. 6. "Gentiles" are fellow heirs, along with Jews. "Gentiles" are members of the same body, along with Jews. "Gentiles" have a share in the same gracious promise of God.

Since the word translated "Gentiles" is cognate to our word "ethnic," much in use today, it seems appropriate to think about the ethnic sensibilities (and sins) of one's own congregation. A fine springboard for such reflection is Flannery O'Connor's short story "Revelation." A new vision comes to Mrs. Turpin while she is out hosing down the hogs at the end of a trying day. She sees white trash and niggers and freaks and lunatics marching into heaven ahead of people like herself, who have always been for "good order and common sense and respectable behavior."

GOSPEL: MATTHEW 2:1–12

The soporific effect of overfamiliarity casts itself over this narrative as well. For many people the reading is so intertwined with old carols like "We Three Kings of Orient Are," and with scenes from Menotti's *Amahl and the Night Visitors* or from bathrobed kings in the Sunday school pageant that no one hears it afresh. They are surprised if you point out to them that the text itself never calls the wise men "kings" and never tells us how many there were. Presumably two people or five or fifteen are equally capable of bringing the three specified gifts.

What the preacher can do to release the power of this pericope is to be faithful to the narrative. This is story theology. Let it stand in story form. Think about the place Matthew assigns to it in his Gospel, and why. Think about the characters in the story—Herod and the Magi, the child and Mary his mother. Then, but only then, think about the symbolism in the tale—the star, the gifts, the dream.

This legend serves a dual purpose for Matthew. The term "legend" need not make anyone nervous. By definition it is a neutral term. It refers simply to an event purporting to be historical but one which is incapable of verification. We can no more summon eyewitnesses to the Epiphany at Bethlehem than we can summon eyewitnesses to young George Washington chopping down a cherry tree. In this case, however, as Raymond E. Brown observes, the obstacles to historicity are nearly insuperable. The Matthean infancy narratives serve Matthew's theological interests. Throughout the first two chapters of his Gospel he presents Jesus as one who fulfills prophecy. He also presents Jesus as one who upsets expectations. This story does both.

As the opening genealogy has already shown, Jesus is an heir of Abraham, a second Moses, and a second David. Like Moses he comes out of Egypt. Like David he is born in Bethlehem. This story underlines his Davidic roots and provides a reason for getting him down to Egypt.

At the same time, the Jesus in this story is not merely the one who is "born to be king of the Jews" (v. 2). He is emphatically a child. One cannot but hear the words of Isaiah, "and a little child shall lead them" (11:6). That was a prophetic expectation, yes, but not one taken very seriously by those Jews who had an exclusively royal image of the Messiah. Small children are unlikely messianic figures. Matthew is, I think, fully aware of the subtleties of his redaction of this narrative.

Furthermore, this child is one who numbers several non-Jews among his forebears, as the genealogy makes clear. And here in this story he is recognized and given homage by foreigners, but not by the Jewish leaders. In short, for Matthew, Jesus is a very Jewish Messiah, but one with a built-in difference. This subtle almost-but-not-quite message of the Matthean infancy chapters leads in subsequent parts of the Gospel to passages that support charges both that Matthew's is the most Semitic of the Gospels and the most anti-Semitic. This story helps prepare the reader for one of two principal reactions to Jesus—homage or rejection.

The characters in the story deserve attention, as well as the context. Four chief parties are noted. They come in pairs. The Magi are wholly admirable figures. They are probably intended to be thought of as Babylonian astrologers. So greatly did they enrich Christian imagination that later tradition gave them names and dates of death. And their relics reached Cologne, we are told, by the year 1162!

Herod, on the other hand, is prince of duplicity in this account. The poor man duly deserved the epithet "the Great" for his political achievements, but this and similar Gospel stories have tarred him with infamy. In this passage, it is important to note how "greatly perturbed" he and all Jerusalem were by the whole affair. The Epiphany of Jesus was and is and should be deeply disturbing.

The implicit power and might of the Magi and Herod meet their antithesis in Mary and the child. Mary, be it noted, is in a house in Bethlehem, not a stable. And the child may be as much as two years old, if one takes seriously Matt. 2:16. In context, our passage follows the naming of the child. He is Emmanuel, God with us. Far too often the emphasis is placed on the first term of that translation. We need to look at the "us" side of the predication.

In Renaissance art a new emphasis appears in paintings of "The Adoration of the Magi," an emphasis with major christological implications. For example, the child before whom the eldest Magus kneels in Ghirlandaio's 1487 "Adoration," now in Florence, is holding aside his own loincloth. The epiphany there is of Jesus' full humanity. He is completely a male child. The old man reverently touches him as if to make sure of it.

Such paintings help combat the rampant docetism of many congregations. We need to make Mary fully human, too. In this narrative, she is merely the passive representative of the powerless. Yet Matthew in his genealogy deliberately put her in the company of such disreputable figures as Rahab and Bathsheba. Her full humanity deserves equal time.

The Baptism of Our Lord
The First Sunday After the Epiphany

Lutheran	Roman Catholic	Episcopal	Pres/UCC/Chr	Meth/COCU
Isa. 42:1–7	Isa. 42:1–4, 6–7	Isa. 42:1–9	Isa. 42:1–7	Isa. 42:1–9
Acts 10:34–38	Acts 10:34–38	Acts 10:34–38	Acts 10:34–43	Acts 10:34–38
Matt. 3:13–17	Matt. 3:13–17	Matt. 3:13–17	Matt. 3:13–17	Matt. 3:13–17

That "Go-between God," the Holy Spirit, glues these three readings together. Each of them speaks of God's gift of the Spirit to human spirit. Since in many congregations there may be actual baptism on this Sunday, the preacher may wish to emphasize the powerful presence of the Spirit with all baptized, as well as that Spirit's special relationship with Jesus of Nazareth. The scope of the Spirit's activity in these lections permits and encourages such a wide-angle lens.

FIRST LESSON: ISAIAH 42:1–7

Since 1892 this passage, or at least the first four verses of it, have been designated as the first of four Servant Songs embedded in the poetic work of Second Isaiah. The Songs have evoked much speculation about their meaning and especially about the identity of the Servant. For the Christian, however, they are forever wedded to the figure of Jesus. That identification goes back to New Testament times certainly and very possibly to Jesus' self-understanding of his own ministry and mission. It is therefore both legitimate and inevitable for us to read them with Jesus in mind.

The speaker in this poem is clearly the Lord. He calls upon us to look at his Servant. And what do we see? A person clothed in God's Spirit. A person therefore with a passion for justice. A person therefore who doesn't throw his own weight around, and one who doesn't trample on the poor and the oppressed. This is a person, in fact, who is dear to the heart of liberation theologians in every generation.

The two references to spirit in the passage are noteworthy. The Lord's completed action of putting his Spirit on the Servant gets a slightly different shade in the Anchor Bible translation: "I *set* my spirit upon him" (v. 1). To a professor that phrasing conjures up the image of an academic hood solemnly draped over the shoulders of those who are given new status at every graduation. That is perhaps a modern parallel to the prophetic mantle Elijah cast upon Elisha (1 Kings 19:19). It is a garment symbolic of responsibility, authority, and power. Such is the force of God's conferring his Spirit on the Servant. But in v. 5, where the universal creative activity of God is proclaimed, the word spirit appears again. And this time it refers to the human spirit which is everyone's gift from God. We have breath, we have life because all of us are inspirited by God.

The Servant is going to bring forth and establish justice (*mishpat:* vv. lc, 3c, 4b). In this context, as elsewhere in the prophets (cf. Amos 5:24, e.g.), justice is not primarily a juridical concept. It is cognate to righteousness and peace, to that positive quality of life indicated by the biblical word *shalom*. This justice is for the whole earth (v. 4). The song tells us that the Servant won't burn out before he has made it global. Even the coastlands, which for ancient Israelites indicated remote ends of the earth, will be eagerly longing for this *torah*, this guidance.

Verses 2–3 use metaphoric language which poses problems for some people today. One need not assume from v. 2 that the Servant is going to engage only in private conversation and never speak in public. Rather it suggests that he is not going to employ the techniques of a demagogue, ranting and raving to arouse mob fervor. Similarly the bruised reed and the dim wick of v. 3 indicate that this Servant is going to be gentle with the physically wounded and with the psychically feeble. Both dimensions of human suffering are suggested again in v. 7 when the Servant is described as one who will give sight to the blind and freedom to the imprisoned.

One final observation about this reading is in order. In the last reading from Isaiah, we encountered the great Epiphany of Christ as the Light of the world, with contrast between that light and our darkness. Here it is again, in a powerful pair of images of the dark— blindness and a dungeon. Pastoral sensitivity dictates that anyone having a blind person in the congregation deal gently with the first image. And modern penal institutions, at least in this country, usually provide some kind of lighting. But one should not dismiss these powerful metaphors too easily. By exploring them imaginatively, one might well open up to new light the depths of hungering darkness all of us share but seldom talk about.

SECOND LESSON: ACTS 10:34–38

As it stands, this short extract from Peter's speech to the Roman centurion Cornelius and his household in Caesarea is undoubtedly intended to build a two-lane bridge between the Servant Song and the account of Jesus' baptism that will follow. The "light of the nations" theme is repeated in Peter's opening line. The decisive nature of Jesus' baptism as the beginning of his public ministry in the power of the Holy Spirit is announced in Peter's second sentence.

Unfortunately the snippet offers no clue as to why Peter "opened his mouth" to say what he said. The congregation deserves to be reminded of the dramatic events recounted in Acts 10 as a whole.

Unless people are freshly aware of Peter's prayer-time vision of that sheet full of all kinds of creatures, all of which are cleansed by God, and unless they are freshly aware of Cornelius's own experience in prayer also, they will miss the point of this reading. It would be appropriate for the lector at least to summarize those events briefly before starting this reading. It would certainly be tempting, especially if one were preaching on the Holy Spirit, to expand the reading to include what happened to the people while Peter was speaking, as well.

For those who do not feel free to tamper with the lectionary, however, these five verses by themselves present ample challenge. Peter's discovery that God "shows no partiality" is shared by Paul, using the same phrase in Rom. 2:11 and Gal. 2:6. The insight was part of their own Jewish heritage. God's impartiality is asserted in Deut. 10:17, for example. God can't be bribed. The English word "impartial" may connote a regrettable, aloof coolness for some hearers, however, which is absent from other contemporary paraphrases of this verse. Both "God has no favorites" (NEB) and "God treats all . . . on the same basis" (TEV) express the same idea more forcefully.

The passage offers at least three additional insights into how God acts. He *sent* good news of peace by Jesus Christ (v. 36). The peace here emphasized is not merely absence of war as the word suggests in classical Greek. Rather it suggests that full well-being of whole persons living in harmony with one another which is the positive richness of the biblical idea of *shalom* we alluded to above. Such an understanding of peace is reinforced when Peter speaks of what Jesus did (v. 38). He healed all that were "oppressed by the devil." Healing includes being freed from both physical and spiritual bondage when one speaks of the good news of peace.

God also *anointed* Jesus (v. 38) with the Holy Spirit and with power. The language of anointing with the Spirit is used also in Isa. 61:1, the passage quoted in Luke 4:18 before the sermon at Nazareth which defines Jesus' liberating mission. The Anointed One is by definition, of course, the Messiah, the Christ.

God therefore and thereby *accompanied* Jesus. God "was with him." This kerygmatic summary on Peter's lips in Acts antedates the development of the doctrine of the trinity, needless to say, but it is in fact a highly trinitarian passage. It offers grounds for theological reflection on the work of the Holy Spirit as "unitive Being" or, more colloquially but still reverently, as God-the-glue.

The account of Jesus' baptism in Matthew differs from the other Synoptics in several significant details. All three agree, however, in interpreting this event as an epiphany, a manifestation of the God made present in Jesus the Christ.

The major difference in this account is the dialogue between John and Jesus in vv. 14–15. It is not found in Mark or Luke. As Matthean redaction, it offers a glimpse of theological concerns special to the first evangelist. Here only Jesus responds with the troublesome answer, "Let it be so for now. . . . "

Two early Christian problems lie behind this exchange, and we need to look at both of them. First, the early church had to cope with the relationship between the followers of John and the followers of Jesus. To the credit of the latter, they did not suppress the fact that Jesus was baptized by John; perhaps it was too well known for them to try. But they felt compelled to explain it, if not to explain it away. Verse 14 reflects that need. Second, Jesus was believed from very early times to have been "without sin." Why then was he participating in a baptism of "repentance for the forgiveness of sin" (Mark 1:4)? Matt. 3:15 proposes an answer.

This is the first time that Jesus speaks in this Gospel. His single sentence contains two key terms in the Matthean vocabulary, "to fulfill" and "righteousness." Donald Senior, in his commentary on this Gospel, suggests that Matthew is, in effect, announcing his interest in God's justice (that is, his saving activity on behalf of his people) and in our response. Obedience to the will of God is the dominant color in the portrait of Jesus that Matthew paints. Other commentators have suggested that "fulfilling all righteousness" is equivalent to fulfilling the Scripture, and have pointed to the idea of baptism in the Red Sea as understood in 1 Cor. 10:2, for example; but this seems farfetched.

Whatever redactional interests are served by this sentence, I find it impossible to consider it an authentic attitude, much less an authentic utterance, of the historical Jesus. It would make his baptism a charade, a bit of play-acting for some ulterior motive. I have to grant that such a conviction intensifies the problem of what Jesus was about, however. So how are we to understand Jesus' baptism in relation to his needing no repentance?

Paul provides a clue in 2 Cor. 5:21, I think: "For our sake he made him to be sin who knew no sin. . . . " Jesus' identification with the human race was so complete that he did, indeed, have a felt need for repentance. As fully human he was fully involved in the corporate sin, the systemic sin, of his generation. He could not escape sharing responsibility for, say, slavery in Palestine any more than we can escape responsibility for, say, racism in America.

The other differences between Matthew's baptismal account and the other Synoptics are in the voice from heaven and the appearance of the Spirit. Mark presents the event in such a way that it could be interpreted as Jesus' private experience. He alone heard the voice and he alone saw the Spirit. Not so in Matthew. This is a dramatic and fully public revelatory moment. The voice says not "*thou* are" but "*this is* my beloved Son." (The language echoes that of our first lesson, Isa. 42:1.) The Spirit that simultaneously descends on Jesus is still a simile, "like a dove" in Matthew; only Luke insists on its bodily form. But for Matthew this Spirit is explicitly "the Spirit *of God*," instead of just "the Spirit" (Mark) or "the Holy Spirit" (Luke).

Because this event in Jesus' life was so pivotal, according to New Testament witness, some commentators have likened it to an ordination for his ministry. In today's church we might quite properly embrace that idea, provided that we insist upon the fact that every baptism is an ordination to ministry. The gift of the Holy Spirit given to all Christians in and through baptism sends all of us out to a ministry of servanthood and empowers us for the job.

The twelfth-century Abbess, Hildegard of Bingen, one of the most accomplished composers, spiritual writers, physicians, and church politicians of her century, thought of herself in ministry as "a feather on the breath of God." That haunting phrase, which serves as the title of a recently released record of Hildegard's music, links together the two major symbols in all accounts of baptism—that of "holy bird," the dove, and of spirit understood as breath or wind of God. A third major symbol needs to be recognized, however—the symbol of water. It is so obvious to us that water flowed in the Jordan River that we could easily overlook its symbolic import in today's Gospel.

Water, like fire, is an inexhaustible religious symbol. It has that bipolar quality indigenous to the holy. It plays a life-or-death role in your life and mine. Any preacher who elects to address the symbol of water on this baptismal occasion would find great help in Helen Keller's autobiography, when she recounts her discovery of the meaning of W-A-T-E-R. One should also consult the appropriate paragraphs in the World Council of Churches Lima Report, *Baptism, Eucharist and Ministry.* One might also meditate on Gen. 8:6–12.

The Second Sunday After the Epiphany

Lutheran	Roman Catholic	Episcopal	Pres/UCC/Chr	Meth/COCU
Isa. 49:1–6	Isa. 49:3, 5–6	Isa. 49:1–7	Isa. 49:3–6	Isa. 49:1–7
1 Cor. 1:1–9	1 Cor. 1:1–3	1 Cor. 1:1–9	1 Cor. 1:1–9	1 Cor. 1:1–9
John 1:29–41	John 1:29–34	John 1:29–41	John 1:29–34	John 1:29–41

In all three of the readings this morning, God calls people out. God also sends people out, that his light may reach to the end of the earth. God also invites us in. He offers strength and companionship. The preacher's task today is to help people think more deeply about Christian vocation and Christian mission.

FIRST LESSON: ISAIAH 49:1–6

As the second of the well-known Servant Poems in Second Isaiah, this passage is linked with the first (Isa. 42:1–6), which was read last week. In this one there is no ambiguity about the identity of the Servant, however. He is explicitly named as Israel in v. 3, and arguments that this is a gloss are not conclusive. The exegete must therefore not just glibly transfer this poetic message to Jesus. A corporate body is being called and sent and upheld.

The calling is no whim on God's part. He called this Servant before birth. He named the Servant while it was still a fetus. That calling in v. 1c is in parallelism with the naming in v. 1d. Our individual assignments in life as well as our corporate ones are never random accident.

In this poem the sending is as a gift to all the nations—to those people from afar invoked in the opening line. An assignment merely to bring the nation Israel back into relationship with the Lord is too limited in scope. God makes his Servant an agent of salvation for the whole globe.

The kind of companionship offered in the Servant's experience is expressed most sharply in the idiom of hiding. The Servant is hidden in the shadow of the Lord's hand (v. 2a). He is hidden away in the Lord's quiver (v. 2b), anonymous in the crowd of identical arrows. Two different Hebrew words are translated "hid" in this one verse, but the context gives the different nuances. We can easily identify with both. In v. 2a we hear the strong word of protection. The "shadow of God's hand" is a mighty metaphor both of protection and of coolness in the heat of the day. In v. 2b we recognize our own yearning to get lost in the crowd, so that we won't have to recognize and respond to the call with our own name on it.

The two ideas of hiddenness suggested here are related to the two conflicting emotions that the Servant articulates in v. 4. In the first half of that verse he is despairing. Does he want to hide again in the quiver on God's back? But in the second half the protecting hand wins out. The Servant is energized by the fact that he has "recompense with my God."

Scholars are uneasy about the next verse. It is probably out of place and needs relocation to give the passage greater coherence. One suggestion is that v. 5c needs to be transposed so that the Servant accepts strength from the Lord before hearing the Lord's commission to go forth as a light to the nations. Whatever one thinks of this emendation of the text, a contrast of strengths carries the final verses.

The Servant thinks he has spent *his* strength "for nothing and vanity" (v. 4). The double negative underlines utter emptiness. What can be more nothing than nothingness? But then the text tells us that the Servant discovered *God's* strength—in a new and personal relationship: "And my God has become my strength." In that strength, the Servant can launch out to the ends of the earth.

SECOND LESSON: 1 CORINTHIANS 1:1–9

This opening passage of 1 Corinthians begins a sequence of readings from that letter which will continue until the last Sunday of the season. Some preachers might therefore wish to plan a series of sermons based on what Paul has to say to that specific first-century Christian community—and therefore to us. These comments will continue to focus, however, on what seems to be the theme common to all of the readings for a given Sunday.

In this passage, the theme of calling which pervaded the Servant Song is as loud and as insistent as a bugle. Paul has been called. The Christians in Corinth have been called—both called out and called together. And again God is the one who issues the call, both to Paul and to the church as a whole.

Paul almost always mentions fellow writers. His colleague Sosthenes may have been the same person mentioned in Acts 18:17 as the ruler of a synagogue in Greek territory. Paul designates his own calling succinctly. He has been called to be "an apostle of Christ Jesus." Later in this letter Paul says that he is unfit to be called an apostle because of his former persecution of the church (15:9); but in other parts of the Corinthian correspondence he defends his work as that of "a true apostle" (2 Cor. 12:12) as opposed to deceitful counterfeits. The term "apostle" should be rescued from its appropriation to the Twelve in our minds, and given verbal force. Like the Servant, Paul is one who is sent.

The community of Christians to whom he writes is called "to be holy." This term also needs refurbishing in modern ears. No moralism is implied. The Corinthians are simply called to be God's people. Paul never uses the word "saint" in the singular. And it soon becomes clear in this letter that these Corinthians wear no halos in Paul's eyes. The communal nature of the calling to be saints is explained more fully at the end of this reading. It is a call to *koinonia* (v. 9). God called them "into the fellowship of his Son Jesus Christ." This does not mean called into a local club of the like-minded. It means at the very least a partnership, a bonding among all people everywhere who "call on the name of the same Lord." The word *koinonia* is many-dimensioned. It is not enough to say with the RSV that one is called into "fellowship." You need to ring changes on that tired word.

Because Paul's letter begins in the conventional form of polite letter writing in the first century, we can easily miss the astounding claims he makes in the "thanksgiving" section which follows the salutation. Those Christians in Corinth have been enriched by Christ "in every way'' (v. 5). No spiritual gift of any kind is lacking among them (v. 7). Collectively they can count on the Lord to stick with them and to keep on blessing them richly until the end. Paul seems certain that these people share with him that tiptoe expectancy with which he signs his name at the end of the whole letter: ''Our Lord, come!'' (16:22).

God's call does not, of course, come to any congregation or to any individual by long-distance telephone. Yet in this passage we are assured not only that he has called, but that (to strain the metaphor a bit) the phone may ring again any minute. Busy people, the clergy not least among them, often hope that the phone will never ring again. Yet anticipation of a call from someone you love arouses all of your senses to a keen pitch. Your ears are alert. So is the rest of you. Paul's use of the word ''call'' in this reading invites us to be ready for *that* ring.

GOSPEL: JOHN 1:29–41

In this reading we encounter the way the Fourth Evangelist deals with the problem we discussed last week in relation to the Matthean account of Jesus' baptism; namely, how the followers of John the Baptizer are related to those of Jesus. We are given no direct account of the baptism but we are told forcefully that John identified the Christ for his own disciples, and that they promptly turned and followed Jesus. The function of John the Baptist in this Gospel is to reveal to Israel the true nature of the Christ.

John the Baptist does this by giving his own eyewitness testimony that he himself saw the Holy Spirit descend and remain on Jesus. He does this also by twice commanding people to behold the Lamb of God. Both forms of identification use language that is of great importance in the Fourth Gospel. We need to look at each of them.

The Spirit would descend ''and remain'' on someone, John had been told. He reports that he saw just that. The Spirit descended on Jesus and ''it remained on him'' (v. 32). The verb ''to remain'' (*menein*) is a favorite of the author of this Gospel. He uses it forty times. The word, variously translated also ''stay,'' ''dwell on,'' ''abide,'' suggests that permanence of the divine as distinct from the temporary character of much of human life. The Johannine writings also use it to express the divine indwelling in Christians, and the fact that Christians must abide in light, love, truth, and the teaching of Christ.

Not only does the Baptist emphasize the fact that the Spirit stayed on Jesus. He also twice repeats the christological title "Lamb of God," one familiar to many music lovers in its Latin form, *Agnus Dei*. Commentators debate the question of whether we are to understand the title here against the background of Isa. 53:7, where the Suffering Servant is "like a lamb that is led to the slaughter," or against the background of the Paschal Lamb (cf. 1 Cor. 5:7). After weighing the evidence for each option carefully, Raymond E. Brown wisely concludes in his Anchor Bible commentary that the evangelist probably intended both references.

A third possible source of the "Lamb of God" title is in apocalyptic thought, which used the figure of a conquering Lamb, as in Rev. 17:14. This possibility is only likely if one thinks that these verses represent the theology of the historical John the Baptist rather than that of the Johannine redactor, however; and I do not.

When the two disciples hear the call, "Behold, the Lamb of God! they follow Jesus (v. 37). Jesus invites them to come and see where he is staying. And, we are told, they stayed (*menein,* again) with him. The theological overtones of this assertion are independent of the reported fact that it was late in the afternoon.

In the final verse, the meaning of the word "first" is unclear. It is tempting to understand it to mean "right there and then"; late as it was, Andrew rushed off to find his brother, Simon Peter, before allowing himself to stay with Jesus. On the other hand some exegetes, partly out of an impulse to harmonize this account with the synoptic version of the call of the first disciples, take it to mean that Andrew and the other unnamed disciple both went looking for their brothers; but that Andrew found his first. Given this possible meaning of the word "first," the unnamed disciple is presumably John, the Beloved Disciple. We would then have the first four disciples of tradition— Peter and Andrew, James and John, just as Matthew will tell us next week.

Whatever the force of that word "first," the impact of this verse on centuries of Christian imagination about the call to discipleship has been powerful. Sometimes we hear that call through another person, through a sister or a brother. Whether a blood relative or not, that person announces to us, "We have found the Christ." The next verse puts it simply. Andrew took Peter to Jesus.

I am surprised to find myself recommending a sentimental

nineteenth-century hymn for your reflection. Ordinarily such hymns convey sticky theology in cotton-candy coating. One from that era, however, has been so firmly bonded to a memorable tune that it bursts unbidden out of my childhood in this context, into mind and whistle. The hymn begins, "Jesus calls us, o'er the tumult of our life's wild, restless sea." It continues, "As of old, Saint Andrew heard it. . . ." The author of the hymn was thinking of the synoptic account of the call of Andrew, not the Johannine. We do not know whether Andrew first met Jesus in the trans-Jordan or by the Sea of Galilee. It may be, as tradition tells us, that he was crucified head-down not many years later. But at this point in his life, according to this morning's gospel, he went out and looked for his brother in order to tell him some good news. That, I take it, is the mission of all of us.

The Third Sunday After the Epiphany

Lutheran	Roman Catholic	Episcopal	Pres/UCC/Chr	Meth/COCU
Isa. 9:1b–4 or Amos 3:1–8	Isa. 8:23—9:3	Amos 3:1–5	Isa. 9:1–4	Isa. 9:1–4 or Amos 3:1–8
1 Cor. 1:10–17	1 Cor. 1:10–13, 17	1 Cor. 1:10–17	1 Cor. 1:10–17	1 Cor. 1:10–17
Matt. 4:12–23	Matt. 4:12–23 or Matt. 4:12–17	Matt. 4:12–23	Matt. 4:12–23	Matt. 4:12–23

Some lectionaries give you a choice between two Old Testament readings this week. Perhaps this is because the lesson from Isaiah forms part of the fixed reading on Christmas Day, and repeating it this soon thereafter, shorn of its Christmas crescendo, might be judged confusing. The option from Amos furthermore offers the preacher some vivid figures of speech to enliven the imagination. Yet the Isaiah passage makes a splendid complement to the Gospel, which quotes from it. And it again reiterates the great Epiphany theme of light. I have therefore chosen to focus on that selection and its relation to the Matthew reading.

FIRST LESSON: ISAIAH 9:1b–4

The starting place for this reading is awkward. Verse 1b is a transitional sentence linking what preceded to a new oracle which begins in v. 2 and actually continues through v. 7. The reason for starting with v. 1b is obvious when we come to the quotation of it in Matthew, but the lector will have to supply the subject of the sentence, the Lord.

Some geography and some history are necessary to understand this verse and also v. 4. Zebulun and Naphtali are, of course, two of the tribes of ancient Israel that were part of the earliest confederacy. Both tribes are praised in the "Song of Deborah" (Judg. 5:18) for risking their lives to defend Israelite territory. Both are again mentioned in the account of the battle against the Midianites under the charismatic leadership of Gideon (Judg. 6:35). One should reread the whole of the Gideon story in Judges 6—8 to sense both the horrors of Midianite oppression and the valor of these tribes.

"Contempt" (v. 1b) fell on the territory of those tribes in later centuries in the person of Tiglath-pileser, the Assyrian emperor who overwhelmed the land in 733–732 B.C. The summary of this event in 2 Kings 15:29 explicitly cites Galilee as part of the land of Naphtali, whose citizens were deported. The Assyrian colonial policy is, in fact, responsible for the high percentage of Gentiles in Galilee in Jesus' lifetime. The "way of the sea" in this verse, incidentally, is a poetic designation for the major caravan route from Damascus to the ocean. Nevertheless the verse as a whole remains obscure. Jewish translators simply add a footnote, "Meaning of verse uncertain."

The passage moves then into a prophetic oracle of great joy. The full cause of this joy is not clear in this selection. It is announced in v. 6 in the familiar words, "For to us a child is born. . . ." What we are reading is a portion of a "dynastic oracle," one talking about a king—either on the occasion of an actual royal birth, or of a coronation, or in anticipation of a future messianic sovereign. Christian tradition, needless to say, has chosen that last alternative.

Verse 2 announced an enormous change—from darkness to light, from night to day. The change was not only physical. It had a psychological impact as well. The decisive quality of psychic change is well conveyed by the translation, "those who dwelt in a land of gloom" (JPS). Somehow, "gloom" is always more depressing than "darkness."

Verse 3 then tells us how good things are now, leaving it for v. 4 to tell us how bad they were. Only a poet would have wit to realize how much more powerful this order is. Most of us would describe the bad situation first, expecting it to set the stage for the new joy. Here we find rejoicing and exultation expressed in concrete images. Good harvests always evoke singing and dancing. Presumably, plundering one's victims in war always has, too.

The three metaphors of oppression in v. 4 communicate less clearly in the singular. Although one can see a person now able to stand upright, freed from serving as a beast of burden, freed from beatings, it makes more sense to cast the whole verse in the plural as the JPS has done. The people who walked in darkness have been freed from ''the yoke that they bore,'' ''the stick on their back'' and ''the rod of their taskmaster.'' Why should they not feel lighter and walk more lightly in this new day?

SECOND LESSON: 1 CORINTHIANS 1:10–17

No thematic connections between this and the previous reading are readily apparent, and the preacher would be wise not to force any— although a case might be made that these contentious Corinthians are still sitting in darkness. Anyone choosing to focus on this text would do better to stick with its own historic *Sitz im Leben* and with the glaring similarities to life in our churches today. The major theological thrust is that, for Paul, the cross is central to the gospel. He refuses to sound like a philosopher at the expense of his own deepest conviction.

Taken by itself the passage opens a fascinating window on what life was life for urban Christians more than nineteen centuries ago. Consider Chloe (v. 11). We know next to nothing about her except that she probably had a group of Christians meeting regularly in her house, which argues for some degree of affluence. She was probably some kind of businesswoman, whose traveling representatives brought Paul news of what was going on in that congregation. That is the best reconstruction of the report from ''Chloe's people'' in v. 11.

Consider Stephanas (v. 16). All we know about him is that he had a ''household'' which Paul baptized. A wife? Children? Slaves? How many of each? Doctoral dissertations have probably been written on this verse, because it has been clutched as a straw by people who want to argue for infant baptism as an early Christian practice. On that subject it is totally inconclusive. But imagine what it must have been like to be part of a household that was baptized all together by an itinerant preacher.

What I think is most important for the preacher to communicate— and probably also the most difficult—is that this letter is written to real flesh-and-blood people. They too had to worry about the cost of groceries. They too had aging relatives with terminal diseases. They probably even had rebellious teen-agers determined to sample the night life of Corinth. It was a city with a reputation equal to that of, say, Paris today.

To this fully human bunch of people, Paul writes with no little asperity. He has heard that they are setting up rival camps, claiming that *their* preacher is better than *your* preacher. One can almost hear a gaggle of third-graders taunting each other on the school playground when Paul writes, "*I* belong to Cephas"; "*I* belong to Apollos."

The four names that Paul mentions in v. 12 have provided historical scholars with grounds for much speculation. Had Apollos been in Corinth long enough to gather a coterie of devoted followers? In 3:4 Paul suggests that he was the chief rival in Corinth. Acts 18:11 reports that Paul lived and preached in Corinth for eighteen months. Acts 18 also describes Apollos as an Alexandrian Jew, both eloquent and well-educated in Scriptures. We know he came to Corinth, but we do not know how long he stayed (Acts 19:1). From the few hints that Acts gives us, put together with Paul's touchiness about his own lack of eloquence, one gets the distinct impression that Apollos's reputation as the better preacher rankled with Paul. But this impression goes well beyond the historical evidence of the New Testament.

A party that says it belongs to Peter (Cephas) and another that says that it belongs to Christ are even more problematic. We do not know whether Peter ever got to Corinth, although C.K. Barrett ventures to say that he probably did. It would, of course, be a normal stopover if one were en route to Rome. A party refusing to be a party might well claim just the name of Christ. That interpretation finds support in 3:22–23. There Paul and Apollos and Cephas are merely men but the Corinthians "are Christ's."

The question Paul asks in v. 13a, "Is Christ divided?" is rhetorical. It expects the answer no! Any preacher talking about this text needs to address it, if possible, without cynicism and with profound sensitivity. The divisiveness in the congregation at Corinth (still almost proverbial when 1 Clement was written perhaps a generation later) besets all of our congregations today in one form or another. But it also besets the worldwide church. The reason why this passage is an appropriate Epiphany reading lies, in my judgment, precisely in its global implications. Christ is not divided, and those of us who view him as an agent of light for all nations need to proclaim the fact not only with our lips but in our lives.

Having ridiculed party spirit, Paul then cuts through all the claims of all the factions with his twofold definition of his own ministry: "Christ did not send me to baptize but to preach the gospel" (v. 17a); "And not with eloquent wisdom, lest the cross of Christ be emptied of its power" (v. 17b).

The first half of the verse is not the assertion of an antisacramentalist position but rather the strong assertion that preaching the good news is the top priority for Paul and for his Lord. What is most important in the second half of the verse is the cross.

When we turn next to the Gospel we will see that Matthew there presents Jesus as a teacher, indeed as a teacher of Wisdom. Paul in his polemic against what were probably "proto-gnostics" in the church at Corinth protests too much against eloquence and wisdom. He exhibits both. Yet neither eloquence nor wisdom had, in his judgment, anything to add to the stark fact of the cross of Christ.

In the context of Epiphany, we need, therefore, to think about the light the cross throws on the darkness in our churches and in our world. The centrality of the cross in Pauline theology needs no documentation. Nor do we have room to expound on it here. We do have room, however, to say that if one chooses to preach from this second reading about the power of the cross, one must avoid triumphalism. However high you wish to lift the cross, you must make your congregation remember Beirut and Teheran and Capetown and your town. Millions of people walk in darkness. They have yet to see a great light.

GOSPEL: MATTHEW 4:12–23

Matthew includes three different kinds of material in this transitional section which follows his account of the temptation and prepares us for the Sermon on the Mount. First he makes an extended comment on the place where Jesus began his public ministry. Then he gives a straightforward account of the call of the first disciples, following his Markan source fairly closely. Third, he offers a summary statement of the nature of Jesus' ministry.

The arrest of John the Baptist triggered the start of Jesus' preaching according to both Mark and Matthew. The word Matthew uses in v. 12 to report Jesus' return to Galilee, he "withdrew," is misleading if it is taken to suggest that Jesus was in any sense retreating from possible conflict. Galilee was exactly the territory over which the Herod who arrested John (not to be confused with the Herod of the Magi story) ruled.

Matthew makes a great point of Jesus moving to Capernaum to fulfill prophecy. He is fond of the formula that this or that happened in order that what was spoken by the prophet might be fulfilled. In this case he cites the passage from Isaiah 9 that opened our first lesson. But the text as Matthew gives it is an exact quotation from neither the Hebrew nor the Septuagint. Matthew may have been quoting with a faulty memory. He may have been deliberately paraphrasing. Whatever the case, two differences are noteworthy. The Isaiah "land of deep darkness" has become "the region and shadow of death." The light has not "shined," it has "dawned." John's arrest makes the idea that Galilee was a region under the shadow of death particularly apt. And the idea of the dawn rather than high noon, as it were, fits Matthew's understanding of the new day beginning with Jesus' new activity. "From that time" he began preaching that the "kingdom of heaven is at hand." Apart from the distinctively Matthean phrase "kingdom of heaven" rather than the kingdom of God as in the other Synoptics, presumably to avoid using the divine name, the kernel of Jesus' preaching is the same as that reported by Mark. The kingdom is right over the horizon, just as the sun at dawn.

The call of the first four disciples differs markedly from the account in John's Gospel, as we have already noted. By some deft editing of the Markan material, Matthew manages to highlight the immediate response both pairs of brothers made to Jesus. Verses 20 and 22 sharply emphasize this. The speed with which one answers God's call to discipleship is probably less important an emphasis, however, than the graciousness of the invitation. Almost certainly the early church used this account of people leaping at the chance to be with Jesus in some connection with the parable of the Great Supper (Matt. 22:1-10; Luke 14:15-24). The absurd excuses people come up with (especially in the Lukan version which is less heavily allegorized) are made doubly absurd by the magnitude of the missed opportunity. It is not every day that the king invites you to a marriage feast for his son!

Matthew's own special portrait of Jesus is summarized in the final verse of this reading. For Matthew, Jesus is preeminently a teacher and a healer. These activities supplement the Markan note that Jesus was primarily a preacher of the kingdom. The sentence is repeated almost in identical form at 9:35. But here it serves as a prelude to the next two sections of the Gospel. Jesus is teacher in chapters 5–7. He is healer in chapters 8–9.

Note that Galilee is mentioned again, as it had been in the opening verse. However accurate it might be to speak of "Galilee of the Gentiles" (v. 15), the same territory has an ample number of Jewish synagogues. For Matthew, Jesus is a rabbi.

The interplay between the Galilees in the Gospel and the first lesson warrant thinking about contemporary Jewish-Christian dialogue as a theme for the sermon today. Just as the Pauline reading evokes our ecumenical concern, so also should this section of Matthew deepen our interest in the relations between the church and the synagogue today.

The Fourth Sunday After the Epiphany

Lutheran	Roman Catholic	Episcopal	Pres/UCC/Chr	Meth/COCU
Mic. 6:1–8	Zeph. 2:3; 3:12–13	Mic. 6:1–8	Zeph. 2:3; 3:11–13	Zeph. 2:3; 3:11–13 or Mic. 6:1–8
1 Cor. 1:26–31	1 Cor. 1:26–31	1 Cor. 1:(18–25) 26–31	1 Cor. 1:26–31	1 Cor. 1:18–31
Matt. 5:1–12	Matt. 5:1–12a	Matt. 5:1–12	Matt. 5:1–12	Matt. 5:1–12

Our Gospel reading for this week shifts the emphasis from what Jesus did as the light of the world to what Jesus said about the lives of Christian women and men as they walk in that light. From now until the last Sunday after Epiphany, we will hear much of the Sermon on the Mount. This week that reading is illuminated by a great passage from the prophet Micah and by an eloquent section of Paul's Corinthian letter. Both of the first two readings therefore reinforce the message that Jesus' teaching is in continuity with the prophets of Israel and with its Wisdom tradition.

Someone once joked that the Bible is almost as full of quotations as Shakespeare. The final verse of the Micah passage and the Beatitudes are known to most literate people in our culture, whether or not they have ever met them in the biblical setting. The very familiarity of these readings makes it more difficult for the preacher to help people hear God's Word through them. One might well begin preparation by asking the Lord the question Karl Rahner addressed to God in one of his prayers: "How can I bring my hearers to distinguish between You and me in the frightful mixture of You and me that I call my sermons?"

FIRST LESSON: MICAH 6:1–8

For interpretation of this classic passage, the quintessence of Hebrew prophecy, it does not matter much whether these verses come from the lips of the eighth-century prophet himself or from those of a disciple called Deutero-Micah, at work in the reign of King Jeroboam II about 780 B.C. Yet the strong references to Moses are uncharacteristic of the great eighth-century prophets, Micah and his near contemporaries Amos and Isaiah. This fact among others has led some scholars to date the passage at a later period.

Such a comment is intended not "to give the day a scientific tone," but to root this reading in history where it was born. Micah or his disciple was not giving humanity generalized truths about the nature of pure religion. He was lashing out against the apostasy of a people who had substituted external religious forms for close covenant relationship with the Lord, the source of their being.

The setting for this oracle is an imagined courtroom. The form is a favorite of the prophets. The Lord is the plaintiff, bringing lawsuit against Israel. The prophet acts as his attorney, as it were. The defendant, Israel, has no real answer to the charges.

Witnesses to the trial are the mountains and the hills, the heights and depths of the earth. They are summoned to listen to the divine accusation. The Lord is the spokesperson in vv. 3–5. He demands to know how he could possibly have done any more for his people. He charges them to remember his saving acts in freeing them from slavery in Egypt and in bringing them to the promised land.

Remembering is the way of bringing the past alive in the present, in Old Testament thought, as indeed it is in Christian eucharistic practice to this day (cf., e.g., Joshua 24). Here Israel is bidden to remember once again the pivotal event of the exodus, under the leadership of Moses, Miriam, and Aaron. Then it is commanded to recall the efforts of the Moabite king to stop its progress through his territory. Finally, it is to remember "what happened from Shittim to Gilgal" (v. 5b). Shittim was one of the last campsites before crossing the Jordan. Gilgal, near the city of Jericho, was the first camping spot in the new homeland (cf. Josh. 4:19).

In the light of this recital of God's saving acts, Israel responds (vv. 6–7) with profound recognition that there is no possible way to repay such loving care through sacrifices. The exaggerated details of vv. 6–7 make that point dramatically. Thousands of rams and rivers of oil represent wealth beyond imagining. Even sacrifice of one's oldest son could not repay God.

We should hear the prophet speaking directly to us in the final verse of the reading, and we should listen especially to the verbs. God has *showed* us what is good. His saving acts demonstrate what "good" means. In response to God's goodness, we are called to act. The three verbs are not describing pious attitudes. They insist that we should *do, love,* and *walk.* We are to be on the move. Doing justice, loving *ḥesed,* and walking in God's company are really three different ways of saying the same thing. Neither "kindness" nor "mercy" is an adequate translation of *ḥesed.* It denotes that covenant relationship best rendered by "steadfast love," that enduring kind of love that is God's own way of acting.

Human analogies are useful in helping people enter into the meaning here, but it is always a good idea to use more than one human analogy on every occasion. Specifically, in this instance, the analogy of friendship is as powerful and as appropriate as that of parental love. God has been Israel's friend. Israel is called to demonstrate responsive friendship in an adult manner—acting responsibly in all human relationships as well.

SECOND LESSON: 1 CORINTHIANS 1:26–31

Paul makes a major contrast in this section of his letter between human standards of judgment and God's. He does this with rhetorical passion and skill. Three pairs of terms are used as antitheses. The preacher should think carefully about all six words, but the use you make of them in the sermon will be determined by how they relate to your particular congregation.

Because of his firsthand knowledge of the Christians in Corinth, Paul can say easily, and presumably truthfully, that they did not have much wisdom or power or social standing. In many a congregation of Christians in the Western world today, one could not say that. If you are preaching to a highly educated group of men and women (some of whom might even be wise), you will have to come to terms with that fact. Your hearers may include the most powerful people in your community or, indeed, the nation. Perhaps most of the ''best families'' in town attend your church.

These possibilities betray the extent of the suburban captivity of many of our churches, and the degree to which the American dream has overshadowed the revolutionary character of the gospel. People may sing the Magnificat week by week and still believe in their hearts that educational opportunity is the way to power and upward mobility. Success is still measured in these terms.

But God, says Paul, is on the side of the foolish, the weak, and the lowly. Mary said much the same thing, and Hannah before her (cf. Luke 1:46–55 and 1 Sam. 2:1–10). Few of us have been taught to value foolishness, weakness, or being among those whom other people look down on. We would run the risk of being thought un-American were we to embrace such values.

This passage, along with much of the rest of Scripture, turns things radically upside down. Such reversal of standards has, of course, strong political implications. In the light of the first and third readings, however, the preacher may wish to link those reversals more closely to the quality of life of people who ''walk humbly'' with their God and to the ''poor in spirit.''

This direction of thought fits in with Paul's own stress on boasting. The word is not altogether functional for our ears. We have been taught from childhood that boasting is at least impolite. Yet the word ''boasting'' is sharper, rightly more abrasive, than the related term ''pride,'' as in the NEB translation of v. 29, ''And so there is no place for human pride in the presence of God.''

C.K. Barrett translates v. 31, ''If anyone is to glory, let him glory in the Lord.'' For Paul, ''as it is written'' always means in Scripture. He is here quoting a favorite text from Jeremiah, one he cites again in 2 Cor. 10:17. It comes from Jer. 9:24 in the Septuagint. Go reread that passage in the prophet, because it contains all of the themes of wisdom and riches and power about which Paul talks here. In fact Barrett makes the charming suggestion that Paul might even have been drawing on a sermon he had earlier preached in a synagogue when that Jeremiah text was the appointed lection. The art of reworking sermons may go back a long time.

Translating the quotation in this fashion has an added advantage. The Greek text reads "*in* the Lord." Thus instead of boasting *of* God, we are being invited to find our power and wisdom and place in the scheme of things *in* Christ, where Paul has already said we now live (v. 30).

GOSPEL: MATTHEW 5:1–12

Before addressing the text of this reading as such, we need to do two preliminary tasks. We must locate the reading for this and subsequent Sundays in the context of Matthew's Gospel as a whole. We must also make some theological observations about the Sermon on the Mount as a whole.

Matthew's Gospel has often been called a handbook for Christian teachers. It is arranged in sections with collections of sayings or "discourses" alternating with deeds or "mighty works." There are five discourses, often thought to be in intentional imitation of the five books of the Torah. Given this comparison, and especially in light of the setting on "the mountain" in 5:1, Matthew appears to be presenting Jesus as a second Moses now giving a new Torah from another Sinai. Many details in the Gospel support this hypothesis—most markedly Matthew's account of the "flight into Egypt," which makes Jesus, like Moses, one who came out of Egypt. Not all contemporary redaction critics find this old version of Matthew's intention fully adequate, of course; but I think it still serves as a useful working hypothesis because it illumines so much of Matthew 5—7.

Such a very generalized picture of the evangelist's intention compounds the theological problem, however. If Matthew wants us to think of Jesus as a new Moses, giving us a new law, aren't we confronted with an intolerable perfectionist ethic? The answer must be no, and for two reasons. The first is quite simple. Christians have long labored under misunderstanding of the Jewish idea of Torah. It does not mean "law" in any legalistic sense at all, but rather something closer to God's gracious guidance of and for his people. In this light, the Sermon on the Mount offers further gracious guidance.

The second reason for rejecting the notion that we are here burdened with an impossible demand for perfection is equally simple. Matthew 5—7 is written in the light of the gospel. Joachim Jeremias made this decisive point forcibly in an article on the sermon published over twenty years ago, and since reprinted in pamphlet form by Facet Books (Fortress Press, 1973). Jeremias reached a conclusion that we would do well to take as a presupposition: "The Sermon is not law, but gospel." The gift of God precedes his demand, and our evangelist knew that full well. Matthew's convictions about the good news of Jesus' death and resurrection, his deep appropriation of the good news of justification, undergird his picture of Jesus as the teacher of a new righteousness.

Taking this perspective with us, we turn now to the text of 5:1–12. The first two verses set the stage. Jesus goes up the mountain. The same word can be translated either hill or mountain, and any tourist who has been to Israel knows that there are no mountains properly so called in Galilee. But this hill carries a definite article. An allusion to *the* holy mountain is surely present. Jesus sits down and begins to teach his disciples—a group of unknown size but clearly contrasted with "the crowds." This teaching is for those who have already committed themselves to follow Jesus.

The next nine sentences (vv. 3–11) begin with the word translated "blessed" or "happy." Eight of these are in more poetic, more rhythmic form than the last—hence the supposition that v. 11 was a later addition, in more prosaic form, to an earlier collection of eight "beatitudes" arranged for easy memorization. Six contain an assertion about the present and a promise for the future. Two are in present tense.

To combat the futurist eschatology of many modern Christians, the preacher would do well to emphasize the two that support the "already" dimension of an inaugurated kingdom. The people to whom the kingdom belongs, as in the first and the last of the eight beatitudes, are the people who know they are poor in spirit, and those who are persecuted. This sandwiching of the present around the future is suggestive. You and I belong to the kingdom now if, for righteousness' sake, we arouse opposition or if we have a true self-understanding in relation to God. And other dimensions of blessedness follow.

That wording, "those who know that they are poor in spirit," is the shameless paraphrase of TEV, not a proper translation at all. Ordinary exegesis of this verse contrasts it with the Lukan parallel in his "Sermon on the Plain," where the blessed are the literal poor. It often deplores Matthew's spiritualizing (for which read "watering down") of this beatitude. But by introducing the idea that what matters is whether people know of their own bankruptcy, the TEV has, in my judgment, entirely rescued us from equating "poor in spirit" with a Uriah Heep type of ostentatious humility, everlastingly forcing itself on the consciousness of others, as that clerk did in *David Copperfield*.

The characteristics of these happy Christians to whom these abundant promises attach themselves invite us to look into a kaleidoscope. The pattern changes slightly from verse to verse, but the bright colors remain constant. Most of the terms require some revitalization. Most women do not wish to be promised to be called "sons of God," and the preacher could emend that phrase to read "children of God." Meekness (v. 5), to take another example, can easily sound like spinelessness to modern ears, whereas "gentleness" does not. The cumulative effect of the Beatitudes is to portray both a great inheritance and heirs worthy of that kingdom. Yet the preacher probably needs to focus on one or another of them. In the light of the earlier readings, "the poor in spirit" seem to deserve that concentration.

The Fifth Sunday After the Epiphany

Lutheran	Roman Catholic	Episcopal	Pres/UCC/Chr	Meth/COCU
Isa. 58:5–9a	Isa. 58:7–10	Hab. 3:1–6, 17–19	Isa. 58:7–10	Isa. 58:5–10
1 Cor. 2:1–5	1 Cor. 2:1–5	1 Cor. 2:1–11	1 Cor. 2:1–5	1 Cor. 2:1–11
Matt. 5:13–20	Matt. 5:13–16	Matt. 5:13–20	Matt. 5:13–16	Matt. 5:13–20

As you sit down under the texts to prepare for this Sunday, you will need to take the calendar into account. If Ash Wednesday is almost upon you this year, the first lesson from Isaiah will deserve treatment sharply pointed in that direction. If, on the other hand, you will be continuing the course readings from 1 Corinthians and Matthew for several more weeks, your sermon will be more open-ended. The rhythms of the church year, especially in variable seasons, place extra demands on those who proclaim God's word so that it may help to sanctify time.

FIRST LESSON: ISAIAH 58:5–9a

Again this reading is part of a longer poem comparing two types of worship. The occasion of the poem is suggested in v. 3. The people have evidently asked the prophet why God is not responding to their observance of days of fasting and repentance. He answers in the name of the Lord with a scathing indictment of their fasts. They bow their heads like so many bulrushes, but go right on seeking their own profit. They sit on sackcloth, but ignore the poor.

Such denunciation of merely formal worship divorced from inner change of heart is part of Israel's great prophetic tradition from Amos to Zechariah. We hear again God telling Israel that he hates and despises their feast days and their solemn assemblies (Amos 5:21). We hear again God asking Israel whether their twice yearly fasts were for his sake or their own (Zech. 7:5).

The Lord addresses a series of questions to his people here also. Is not the fast that he chooses far different? Is it not to free the oppressed, to share their bread with the hungry, to bring the poor into their own houses, to clothe the naked? Not only does this insistent demand for social justice trumpet forth from all of Israel's great prophets, but it sounds exactly like the standard of justice the Lord demands in Matt. 25:34–36. Indeed the verbal details of that Matthean passage are impressively close to those of this poem.

One detail of the RSV translation is misleading in this reading. In v. 7b the phrase "not to hide yourself from your own flesh" sounds almost like a charge to take off one's own clothes to cover the naked. The sense of the verse is clearer in the JPS translation, "And not to ignore your own kin"—your own poor relations, one might say today.

In the final two verses a picture of a bright new day that would follow such a true fast is painted in imagery that is a familiar part of the Epiphany season. The Israelites have been crying to the Lord and he has apparently not heard them. But if they observe the fast he chooses, then light shall break forth (v. 8a), healing shall spring up. James Muilenburg suggests that the healing metaphor here literally means the quick growth of new flesh over a raw wound, surely a graphic image of restored wholeness.

In v. 8b the new situation is described in language close to that of Isa. 52:12b, "for the Lord will go before you, and the God of Israel will be your rear guard." The allusion is to the constant companionship of the Lord during Israel's exodus journey, when he went with them by day in a pillar of cloud and by night in a pillar of fire (cf. Exod. 13:21). This needs to be underlined if people are to understand v. 8b rightly. "Your righteousness" deserves at least a capital R. Righteousness is never our own achievement or our own possession according to Christian or Hebraic thought. JPS again makes this clearer than RSV with the translation, "Your Vindicator shall march before you."

Finally we are brought back to the context of worship. However much the prophets are opposed to mere formalism, they are never opposed to worship itself. In the days when the people's fasts were on the surface only, the Lord seemed to turn a deaf ear to their prayers. Zech. 7:13 sums up the same situation in these words of the Lord: "As I called and they would not hear, so they called and I would not hear." But now, Isaiah assures Israel, when they keep the fast the Lord chooses, then they shall call and the Lord *will* answer (v. 9a). He will answer with his presence: "Here I am."

If I were preaching on this passage at this season, I think I would clip my illustrations out of the week's newspapers, including the section announcing church services. If it is about to be Lent, it should not be hard to find plenty of religious activity confined, no doubt, to "the religion page." It is never hard to find real news about the hungry, the homeless, and the hopeless. One should not, of course, clobber the congregation with the obvious. Yet the preacher using a little subtlety could let the local newspaper illuminate the key question in this reading: "Is not this the fast I choose?" (v. 6a).

SECOND LESSON: 1 CORINTHIANS 2:1-5

Paul tells us plainly in these verses that he made a conscious decision about his own preaching strategy and style in Corinth (2:2). The verb he uses can also be rendered "resolved" (NEB) or, more loosely, "I made up my mind" (TEV). What he has to say about that decision remains critical for today's preachers. But the decision is not as simplistic as a casual reading of this passage might suggest.

Before we explore the content of the resolution Paul made, it is worth asking why he decided on this particular way of working. Some commentators have found an explanation in Paul's preaching experience before he reached Corinth. One fanciful way to go is to read Acts 17:16–34, Paul's speech to the philosophers at Athens, as a total flop which led Paul to say to himself, in effect, "Well, I won't try that again!" Unfortunately the Acts text is itself fanciful; and it does not present Paul's venture into philosophy as a complete washout, in any case.

Other commentators link the decision of v. 2 to the state of Paul's physical or mental health while he was in Corinth, to which he himself alludes in v. 3. What was this weakness? We do not know. Hans Conzelmann wonders if Paul were ill. Barrett wonders if his "fear and trembling" were caused by a sense of the heavy responsibility of preaching God's Word. With their own brand of paraphrase, the NEB translators decide he was "nervous" (v. 3). In my own experience, however, and perhaps in yours, the more nervous I am before preaching, the more I am tempted to find and use "plausible words of wisdom" (v. 4).

There may be some truth in both kinds of speculation. After all, which of us ever makes a conscious decision without some unconscious motives also at work? Nevertheless the far more likely cause of Paul's strategy was the religious climate in Corinth itself, one rightly described as "proto-gnostic." Corinthians were attracted to esoteric "knowledge" and "wisdom," secret *gnosis* and *sophia* imparted to the spiritually elite, frequently in embroidered language. In opposition to that kind of religious elitism, Paul nails his message firmly to the cross.

As a result of Paul's decision, his preaching in Corinth was accompanied by a demonstration or manifestation (not "proof," please) of Spirit and power (v. 4). Neither word wears a definite article in the Greek. They are two different words used to express a single concept. As an outcome of this type of preaching, Christian faith rests not in human wisdom but in God.

The issues Paul puts before us in this short paragraph are very much alive today, both for preachers and for their congregations. Two of them are noteworthy. What use do you as a theologian make of contemporary science and philosophy to help you understand and communicate the gospel? What use should you make? That issue was sharply posed earlier in this century. It was answered one way by Paul Tillich, for example, and in another way by Karl Barth. However you resolve it, you should note that Paul of Tarsus lends no support in this letter to any anti-intellectual stance any more than he does to intellectual elitism (cf. 2:6).

Second, to what extent do we appropriate Paul's profound insight, reached centuries before Marshall McLuhan, that "the medium is the message," and therefore adopt his style? Paul recognizes here that what he had to say and how he said it were inseparable. His "speech" and his "message" (v. 4) go together. That is why, I think, he told the story of Jesus Christ without resorting to "lofty words." And that is why we should, too.

GOSPEL: MATTHEW 5:13–20

Jesus certainly never used "lofty words," according to the synoptic record. Rather, he spoke in parables. In this reading we hear two of his parabolic sayings using two of the most mundane aspects of daily life—salt and lamps. We also hear Matthew's understanding of Jesus' attitude toward Scripture.

The saying that the disciples are "the salt of the earth" has a close Lukan parallel (Luke 14:34–35) and so is usually identified as a Q saying; but it and its twin are really parables of "the triple tradition." Mark 9:50 echoes the same idea of tasteless salt, Mark 4:21, the lamp saying. I have read learned commentaries on the salt saying which try to explain to me how it is possible for salt to lose its taste, but the explanations never convince me nor my friends who are chemists. What Jesus is doing here, I am convinced, is using parabolic humor. Unsalty salt is a contradiction in terms. You would indeed throw it out just as quickly as you would pour a bottle of flat ginger ale down the drain.

In the twin parable, the same kind of parabolic humor recurs. If John Dominic Crossan and Marianne Moore are right, as I think they are, in claiming that parables give us imaginary gardens with real toads in them, then we should expect to stumble over the absurd. Here we are invited to envision someone carefully lighting the wick of an oil lamp and then immediately putting a bucket over it to prevent any glimmer escaping. Energy conservationists today would be rightly appalled at such a waste of oil.

The "you are" indicatives of vv. 13 and 14 need to be noted. The "you" are the disciples collectively. Their charge here is to prevent life from being flat and dull. Put positively, their charge is to bring zest and shine to life. In spite of the death-knell given v. 16 by its constant use in many churches to get people to open their wallets, Christians are there charged not to dig out a dollar but to glow. One cannot help but be reminded once again of that shine on Moses' face which came from talking with God.

In the second half of the reading (vv. 17–20), we encounter three minor exegetical problems and at least one major hermeneutical one. We need to note that "the law and the prophets" (v. 17) meant Scripture. The third section of the Hebrew Bible had not yet been canonized. We need to note that both "an iota" and "a dot" refer to infinitesimal matters, to the smallest letter and to what amounts to an accent mark in a Greek text. We need to deplore both Matthew's and his subsequent interpreters' pejorative evaluation of the righteousness of the "scribes and Pharisees," those much misunderstood and falsely maligned leaders of first-century Judaism.

We are left with the interpretative question of what Matthew's Jesus wants us to think about righteousness and the law. It is necessary to stress the evangelist's creative work in this pericope. He has put together four originally independent sayings, and put them together in a manner that reflects the situation of the Christians for whom he was writing. This recognition helps explain the tension of thought here.

On the one hand, Matthew is aware of "false prophets" in the community (cf. 7:15–23). Here and elsewhere throughout his Gospel, Matthew is fighting against such people. They were almost certainly people who believed that the law had been abrogated by Christ's death and resurrection, and who therefore had a libertine or antinomian position in regard to it. When he has this battlefield in mind, Matthew argues loudly for the need to remain constantly obedient to the will of God and to bear fruit. Relaxing the commandments and teaching others to do so is set in opposition to doing them and teaching them. Matthew honors teachers who have integrity.

On the other hand, Matthew is also engaged in polemic against the rabbis of his day. This is the front he is thinking of in v. 17 where he plainly presents Jesus as the one who, in his own person, *is* the fulfillment of Scripture. The end time of Scripture has begun with his teaching.

The Sixth Sunday After the Epiphany

Lutheran	Roman Catholic	Episcopal	Pres/UCC/Chr	Meth/COCU
Deut. 30:15–20	Sir. 15:15–20	Sir. 15:11–20	Deut. 30:15–20	Deut. 30:15–20 or Sir. 15:15–20
1 Cor. 2:6–13	1 Cor. 2:6–10	1 Cor. 3:1–9	1 Cor. 2:6–10	1 Cor. 2:6–13
Matt. 5:20–37	Matt. 5:17–37 or Matt. 5:20–22, 27–28, 33–34, 37	Matt. 5:21–24, 27–30, 33–37	Matt. 5:27–37	Matt. 5:20–37

All three readings for this week make their major points by sharp contrasts. The spokespersons (ostensibly Moses, Paul, and Jesus) all call for reorientation, redirection of our whole way of life. They invite us to make some mature decisions about where we are going and how we are going to get there. In effect, all three together help us see things differently.

FIRST LESSON: DEUTERONOMY 30:15–20

The great contrast in this reading is between life and death, both literally and figuratively. The passage appears as part of the aged Moses' farewell address to the people Israel, as they are about to cross over the Jordan and after he knows that he will not be going with them into the promised land. Historically the "address" is probably an exilic composition of the Deuteronomic school. In fact it shows liturgical roots.

You are preaching on part of an ancient sermon by someone who had the gifts of a powerful orator. Notice the effective repetition of "this day." Four times the preacher summons his hearers to make a decision now. He celebrates today as the time for decision. The passage reaches a stunning climax in v. 19 with the ringing imperative, "Therefore choose life."

Synonymous with the contrast between life and death is the contrast between blessing and curse. We need to remember that in ancient Israel these are what modern linguists would call performative words. What they express they also convey. Once uttered, neither a blessing nor a curse can be recalled. We are here brought into the awesome company of people who take words seriously. Words are instruments of life or death.

Blessing in Israelite thought is usually described, as here, in concrete, incarnate terms. It means long life and a big family. Elsewhere in the Old Testament it means also rich harvest and money in the bank, good health and good humor. The effects of a curse are the opposite. Disease, disgrace, ruin, desolation result—all first cousins of death.

Cursedness awaits a community that decides to worship idols, according to our passage. It awaits all those who choose not to hear the Word of God (v. 17), that very Word as near to everyone as if it were in their own mouth (v. 14). Blessedness awaits the same community if it decides to walk in God's ways, to love and worship the Lord. It will experience that fullness of well-being God wants his people to enjoy.

Human choice is here said to be the key to life or death. The dominant biblical theology from Genesis 2 on affirms genuine human freedom. We are creatures, not puppets. We are free to choose. But you will need to spend your best thought, if you choose to focus on this first reading, on the complexities of all human choices. Ultimately they may have the black or white clarity "Moses" here sees in them. Penultimately our choices are always ambiguous. They are not just a simple matter of deciding which exit we should take from the interstate to get to where we want to go. They are frequently a far more subtle matter of distinguishing among shades of gray. Furthermore, we need to take into account the frightening Freudian theory that most of us have a death wish built into our own psyches. We can readily transpose that idea into the key of sin. How far are we really free to choose blessedness?

SECOND LESSON: 1 CORINTHIANS 2:6–13

Paul's major contrast today is between God's wisdom and ours. In context the same contrast is expressed also as that between God's Spirit and the spirit of this world.

Paul's vocabulary in this section demands careful attention. We need to try to make as precise as possible the meaning of the terms he is using, and also to try to find appropriate modern equivalents for them. We will look more closely at the key words, "wisdom" and "spirit," and then at "the mature" and "this age," as well.

"Wisdom" *(sophia)* is a slippery term in 1 Corinthians. Barrett claims that Paul gives the word four different senses in this letter—two of them bad and two of them good. In last Sunday's reading, Paul wanted to have nothing to do with "wisdom." In this week's, he wants to reclaim the word and to insist that he knows "a secret and hidden" wisdom of God.

Something of the ambivalence Paul feels about wisdom may be suggested by our use of the cognate English words "sophomoric" and "philosophical." Sophomores are, by derivation, wise fools. We apply the adjective to immature persons who think they know more than they do. All of us have met such persons, and they are not always students in their second year of college. On the other hand, we tend to think of philosophers as true lovers of wisdom. The adjective is often applied not to abstract flights of speculation, but to a very realistic attitude toward life.

The Wisdom of God plays an active role in late Jewish thought. *Sophia* was personified as God's agent in creation. She is the subject in such passages as Prov. 8:22–31, where she is beside God when he establishes the heavens and the earth. She is the subject of the hymn in Wisdom of Solomon 7, where she is spoken of as an emanation or effluence from the Being of God. In the Wisdom of Jesus ben Sirach, she is said to have thoughts vaster than the ocean, a purpose "deeper than the great abyss" (24:28 NEB). No one has ever fully known her, fully fathomed her. All such passages played an important role in the development of christological thought in the early church, even before the feminine sophia tradition was absorbed by the masculine logos tradition.

This part of his Jewish heritage was certainly part of Paul's thinking about God's wisdom. He alludes to it plainly in v. 7. You remember that in 1 Cor. 1:24 he said that Christ is "the wisdom of God." Direct borrowing from the Wisdom tradition is even more evident in the christological hymn of Colossians 1.

The terms "Spirit" and "spiritual" pose comparable problems in the vocabulary of 1 Corinthians. Paul walks a tightrope, in fact. He is using language that is open to misinterpretation in a way that makes him sound like a proto-gnostic himself. The secret wisdom God has revealed to the Corinthians through the Spirit, however, concerns spiritual gifts (v. 12). Even here we get an anticipation of Paul's later assertion, in his fuller discussion of spiritual gifts in 1 Corinthians 12—14, that the greatest of them is love. The alleged quotation from Scripture in v. 9 is a misquotation. Paul is remembering partly Isa. 64:4. He summons the idea of those who love God from some other source. But the word love is thus already in his mind when he talks about spiritual gifts.

The word translated "mature" in v. 6 is the same word that is translated "perfect" in Matt. 5:48, part of the Gospel for the seventh Sunday after Epiphany. Paul uses the word again in 1 Cor. 14:20, as well as in Phil. 3:15, Col 1:28, and 4:12. He sees maturity not just as a goal to be pursued, but as a status conferred upon believers through Christ.

Finally, the term "this age" needs to be read in the light of Paul's eschatological framework. The old eon is already passing away. The new eon has begun in Christ. We live already partly in the future. The temporal emphasis is preferable to the spatial connotation of the TEV which translates "this world." That lends support to an unfortunate other worldly understanding of the Gospel. The "rulers of this age" (vv. 6, 8) are more likely to be cosmic demonic powers in Paul's mind than human political figures.

After one works through the vocabulary of this lection, one is drawn to reflect further on the intimate connections between human spirit and Holy Spirit Paul is talking about in vv. 10 and 11. His use of theological analogy is exciting. Human beings know their own thoughts through the exercise of their own spirits. Our "spirits" here are pretty nearly what we would call today our consciousness of self, through our capacity for transcendence and self-examination. Paul applies that insight to God's self-understanding. God's Spirit searches or explores his depths of being even as ours do. Since he has shared with us his own Spirit we have new capacity to understand God, ourselves, and our sisters and brothers. We "have the mind of Christ" (v. 16).

If we take seriously what Paul says in v. 13 (however hard it is to decide how to translate this sentence), we not only have new understanding. We can even talk about it together. The good news of v. 13 seems to me to tie in happily with the revival in many of our churches today of more open conversation about "spirituality." We are being freed from our false religious privatism. We can unashamedly seek "spiritual friends" and help one another grow toward that Christian maturity Paul writes about.

GOSPEL: MATTHEW 5:20-37

The chief contrast in the Gospel is between what was said of old and what Jesus says. Matthew presents six resounding antitheses in this section of the Sermon on the Mount. We hear four of them today. In every case, Matthew's Jesus chops down any hedges people have planted around one or another of the Ten Commandments. All are exposed to the full gale of radical demand. Read in the light of v. 20, repeated from last week, the passage explains what a deeper righteousness means.

Before we look at the contrasts in detail, you should note that nothing whatsoever in the text warrants the gratuitous intrusion of "men" (RSV) or "forefathers" (NEB) in the formula beginning, "You have heard . . . " at 5:21 and thereafter. Even "our ancestors" (JB) is an unnecessary expansion of the plain statement, "You have heard that it was said." No doubt Matthew thought Jesus was talking only to males, as the section on sexual mores makes clear; but you are not. I urge you to be sensitive to this fact lest you "rob the gospel of its power" to speak to all your parishioners.

"You shall not kill." Matthew 5:21 is an exact parallel to Exod. 20:13 and Deut. 5:17, ungarnished by judgment. This ancient prohibition of murder is here blown wide open. It is interpreted so broadly that it includes anger, insults, and epithets in its scope. You can deal a deathblow to your sister or brother by what you feel in your heart or what you spit out from your lips.

Matthew stretches this antithesis by adding two sayings. One has immediate contemporary relevance (5:23-24). Put baldly, it says go make peace with your neighbor before you come to church. The other, a Q saying shared by Luke 12:57-59, may seem to have little relation to our lives today, but if it has to do with our relation to God, it parallels the thought of vv. 23-24.

"You shall not commit adultery." Again we have an exact quotation from the Exodus Decalogue (20:14). What Jesus adds is a little complicated. We are presented in 5:29-30 with sayings which have Markan parallels (Mark 9:43-48) and even Matthean doublets (cf. Matt. 18:8-9). The most apposite part of the expanded interpretation is v. 28. A lustful look amounts to rape. Women who are tired of being regarded merely as sex objects rejoice in this verse, but they are deprived of hearing a comparable indictment of their own sexual sins.

The verses on divorce which follow (vv. 31–32) are a rider on the adultery command. They have a long history in Christian tradition, and one should consult the synoptic parallels for variations. Only Matthew adds the exception clause, here and in 19:9. Only Mark entertains the idea that a woman might instigate divorce from her husband.

We come, therefore, to the fourth antithesis, the third of our commandments: "you shall not swear falsely" (v. 33). Now we do not have a precise quotation from the Decalogue either in Exodus or Deuteronomy, where both prohibit bearing false witness against your neighbor. What we have instead is an apparent prohibition of any kind of oath whatsoever. Understood broadly, this command tells us to speak with honest simplicity under all circumstances. Any kind of deceit is as bad as perjury.

That which should be emphasized here is the clarion, "But I say to you. . . . " Jesus is the one who speaks with new authority and not as the scribes. He is the one who has been made manifest this season as Light of the World, Son of God, Immanuel. He is the one made manifest in this Gospel as an agent of the new.

The Seventh Sunday After the Epiphany

Lutheran	Roman Catholic	Episcopal	Pres/UCC/Chr	Meth/COCU
Lev. 19:1–2, 17–18	Lev. 19:1–2, 17–18	Lev. 19:1–2, 9–18	Lev. 19:1–2, 17–18	Lev. 19:1–2, 9–18
1 Cor. 3:10–11, 16–23	1 Cor. 3:16–23	1 Cor. 3:10–11, 16–23	1 Cor. 3:16–23	1 Cor. 3:10–11, 16–23
Matt. 5:38–48	Matt. 5:38–48	Matt. 5:38–48	Matt. 5:38–48	Matt. 5:38–48

You have an opportunity today to help people come to deeper understanding of their relationship with God and with each other. The ways of the Holy and the ways of love bind all three of the readings together. Your goal might be so to interpret them that they evoke great thanksgiving rather than moral resolution from your people.

FIRST LESSON: LEVITICUS 19:1–2, 17–18

These verses are part of the Holiness Code (Leviticus 17—26), a collection of priestly laws both cultic and ethical, edited by the Jerusalem clergy before the exile. It forms the nucleus of the present book of Leviticus as expanded by Priestly editors during and after the exile. The unifying theme of this section is the holiness of the Lord.

God alone is Holy. The root meaning of the word "holy" *(Qadosh)* is that which is separate. This root meaning is clear in Lev. 20:26, which itself exegetes 19:1–2. The "Holy One of Israel," as Isaiah frequently called God, is "Wholly Other." All other holiness is derivative; it is the gift of the Holy One.

Human encounters with the Holy One evoke awe and worship. They bid us (in the unbeatable biblical image) to take off our shoes. As Rudolf Otto showed in his classic study of such encounters, we are at once drawn as if by a magnet and warned to keep our distance. We tremble in the presence of ultimate mystery.

Only the language of worship can approximate any adequate expression of what holiness entails. That is why Isaiah 6 is an invaluable source for thinking about it. The *Sanctus* in our liturgies derives, of course, from Isaiah's decisive experience in the temple. Psalm 99 is almost as powerful a commentary on the holiness of the Lord. In both Isaiah 6 and Psalm 99, the ethical component of this root religious experience is strong. In the presence of the holy, people realize their sin, their need for forgiveness. They recognize the Lord's love for justice and for righteousness, which is part of his holy being.

Because holiness is not something we work up but rather something God sends down, we can be called a holy people, just as Moses tells Israel in this reading. Because we are participants in his holiness through relationship with him, we are enjoined to act as he acts.

The second pair of verses in the short lection spells out some of the horizontal consequences of our vertical relationship, to use rather rusty spatial metaphors. We need to have a new relationship to our brothers and our sisters—and to ourselves.

Verse 17 is somewhat obscure. It needs to be read in the light of

Ezek. 3:18–19 and Matt. 18:15. What the verse suggests is what we today would call confrontation. True love of neighbor is not flabby. True love of neighbor entails reasoning with him or her. If we shirk that responsibility out of our usual selfish desire to avoid a scene, we "bear sin because of him." We have failed to exhibit the tough love here intended.

Verse 18 seems to offer us a narrow definition of our "neighbor" — one that needs the parable of the Good Samaritan as corrective. But the verse also offers us one of the sanest insights into human nature found in all the scriptures of all the world religions, if I may be allowed that hyperbole. The fact: We love ourselves. This is not the result of the Fall; it is biologically necessary. That is why we are commanded to love our neighbors with exactly the same intensity.

Most of us who profess and call ourselves Christians need to hear the church give us permission to love ourselves, instead of beating our own breasts because we do. Leviticus 19:18 and Jesus do just that. The freeing gift of grace announced in this reading empowers all of us to climb St. Bernard of Clairvaux's "Ladder of Love." The bottom rung is loving yourself for your own sake. The top rung is loving yourself for Christ's sake.

SECOND LESSON:
1 CORINTHIANS 3:10–11, 16–23

Immediately prior to this section of his letter (vv. 5–9), Paul was playing with agricultural imagery to tell the Corinthian Christians what was going on among them. They are invited to think of themselves as God's field. Paul the farmer came along and planted the seed. Then Apollos came along and irrigated the field. But neither one is more important than the other, because only God can make the crop grow.

Now in v. 10 Paul abruptly changes from agriculture to architecture. The Corinthians are now to think of themselves as God's building. God is the architect who handed the blueprints over to Paul. Paul arrived in Corinth and laid the foundation of the building—the foundation of Jesus Christ. Apollos is currently building on the foundation Paul had laid.

The verses that are skipped in this lection ring the changes on the kinds of building materials subsequent builders might use. There is no necessary implication that Apollos is working with wood or straw rather than gold or silver. One gets the impression, however, that Paul is not ready to confer on his rival his own self-designation, "master-builder."

Suddenly the picture sharpens. Paul is no longer talking about an anonymous building. He is talking about the temple, the place where God has chosen to make his name dwell. Immediately we are in the precincts of the holy. All that is left out in front of the temple is, by etymology, profane. And the farther we get into the temple, the closer we are to the Holy of Holies.

The "you" pronouns in vv. 16 and 17 are plural. The Corinthians collectively are God's temple. A good case could be made, therefore, for translating the Spirit's dwelling place as "among you" rather than "in you." Paul has in mind the unity of the Christians at Corinth and the threat that divisive behavior might destroy it. He most emphatically shares the same understanding we met in the first lesson—namely, that God is the Holy One and that only the presence of his Spirit makes the Corinthians holy.

The rhetorical peroration of the last sentence is reminiscent of Rom. 8:38–39. Our reading ends with a bang, not a whimper. Thanks to the immense, unfathomable generosity of God, the Corinthians have everything, literally *everything*. The whole world is theirs and more, too. The three people named (Paul, Apollos, and Peter) are in direct reference back to 1:12. There Paul had mocked them for saying that they *belonged* to one or another of these three preachers. On the contrary, he says here. All three of them *belong* to you. In his final flight of phrases, Paul asserts their freedom from any fetters of time or space. Even the future is theirs. Why? Because they belong to Christ and Christ belongs to God.

Any theologian today who talked about the church with such unqualified indicatives would immediately be charged with the sin of "triumphalism." One cannot preach an exalted doctrine of God's holy, catholic church without deep uneasiness about the sin of the church. Paul is by no means blind to the facts of life in the Corinthian church. He makes that a glaring certainty in 5:9–13. Yet he here lays before them a vision of who they really are because of their relationship with Christ. We sometimes need to be reminded of such unequivocal belonging.

GOSPEL: MATTHEW 5:38–48

The last two of the six antitheses in the Sermon on the Mount give today's Gospel its framework. We heard the first four last week. The preacher bears a special obligation in addressing the familiar formula "You have heard that it was said . . . ," in vv. 38 and 43. Neither one is a direct quotation from the Hebrew Bible. The first does, indeed, have close parallels in Exod. 21:24, Lev. 24:20, and Deut. 19:21, but read in their own setting these provisions in ancient Hebrew law indicate concern for limiting revenge. They show a rough-and-ready sense of justice opposed to excess. Parishioners should hear that. The second, with its directive to hate one's enemies, is without any foundation in Jewish Scripture. Parishioners must hear that.

This dimension of the reading offers a chance, therefore, to continue your campaign against widespread Christian misapprehension about the Old Testament. Many people still believe and say that the God of the OT was a God of vengeance, whereas that of the New is a God of love. You know that is poppycock. You can take this opportunity to demonstrate to others how false this impression is.

After doing your part to combat anti-Semitism, you will want to focus on the breathtaking vision of Christian practice in human relations that is here set forth. In vv. 39–42 we are told how to deal with violence, with threats of lawsuits, with occupying troops, and with beggars. These verses have spawned two idiomatic expressions in English which many people use without the faintest notion that they are biblical in origin. "The other cheek" and "the extra mile" have, alas, become faded metaphors. Try to revive them.

At the height of the civil rights crisis of the sixties, I watched the training of student volunteers who were preparing to go to Mississippi to help with voter registration. Each June morning they took over our well-clipped soccer field on campus, and practiced what to do when they were kicked. The memory of those young women and men curled up in the fetal position absorbing mock kicks has illumined v. 39 for me ever since. So also does the knowledge that two of them were killed.

In historical context, v. 41 refers apparently to the edict of the Roman occupying army in Palestine that any soldier had the right to draft a civilian to carry his pack. You might consult someone in your congregation who has lived under occupation to help you update this. Some of the scenes from the film *The Killing Fields* come to mind when one thinks about what the Vietnamese had to cope with from American troops. Both nonviolence and a double portion of voluntary service are almost impossible to contemplate in such circumstances.

In vv. 43–47 we learn how to deal with persecutors and other enemies. Our love of neighbor must be different in kind from that of tax collectors and pagans. We are to pray for those who are out to exterminate us. We are to reach out in loving openness to everyone, whether we know them or not.

This last injunction, implicit in v. 47, sounds deceptively simple, but it should occasion some serious reflection on the need to respect other people's privacy. Have you ever tried walking down the street in your town saying a cheery "Good morning!" to everyone you pass, whether you know them or not? One does not always meet with warm response. I vividly remember a time when I was a seminarian in New York City. Some friends and I decided that we would not allow ourselves to be dehumanized by the cold, impersonal relations of the big city. So we naively insisted on a human exchange with everyone sitting inside a glass box selling us subway tokens and movie tickets, or collecting our bridge tolls. Not only did we snarl traffic, but discovered that we were violating a self-protective coating apparently essential for survival in such jobs.

The moral of that experience is, I think, the danger of taking these descriptions of how love operates too narrowly, too simplistically. The climax of the Gospel is the awesome comparison of our love with God's. The analogy is made by way of those essential gifts of sunshine and rain. Neither figure of speech can be reduced to the notion that God's love is impartial, because both sunshine and rain are life-giving blessings to everyone. Given that emphasis, the command to be as perfect, as whole as God is, becomes the command for uncalculating love, the kind we have all received.

The Eighth Sunday After the Epiphany

Lutheran	Roman Catholic	Episcopal	Pres/UCC/Chr	Meth/COCU
Isa. 49:13–18	Isa. 49:14–15	Isa. 49:8–18	Isa. 49:14–18	Isa. 49:8–18
1 Cor. 4:1–13	1 Cor. 4:1–5	1 Cor. 4:1–5 (6–7), 8–13	1 Cor. 4:1–5	1 Cor. 4:1–13
Matt. 6:24–34	Matt. 6:24–34	Matt. 6:24–34	Matt. 6:24–34	Matt. 6:24–34

Isaiah and Matthew today offer us magnificently matched affirmations of God's loving care. The Corinthians passage sounds a quite different theme and could only be tied in as a counterpoint to the good news of the Old Testament and Gospel readings, or it could be used separately. Certainly the vivid sights and sounds, the colors and feeling tones of the first and third lections invite us to enter into some imperishable poetry.

FIRST LESSON: ISAIAH 49:13–18

Remind yourself once again of the historical and psychological plight of the people for whom Second Isaiah is writing. The Israelites are still in exile, still separated from the homeland that meant so much more than a geographical location in their tradition. However much their standard of living in Babylon was an improvement over slave conditions in Egypt, they could not resist the comparison. They found themselves unable to sing the Lord's song in a strange land. By the waters of Babylon, they sat down and wept (Psalm 137).

Because he has the prophetic insight to see a new day coming with Cyrus the Persian rising on the political horizon, and because he has the prophetic faith that trusts the Lord's steadfast love, Second Isaiah is empowered to bring hope to his people. Because he has poetic genius, he is able to express that hope in language that straightens shoulders and strengthens hearts. Our passage follows the Servant Song we thought about on the second Sunday of this season and a stanza that depicts a glorious homecoming to Zion through a desert that has acquired, as it were, AAA accommodations.

Our passage opens with a brief hymn of thanksgiving (v. 13). The poet hears all nature singing for joy. Earth and sky join the chorus, because the Lord has comforted his people. Both verbs in v. 13b speak of accomplished action rather than one past and the other future as the RSV says. The JPS version of v. 13b reads, ''And has taken back his afflicted ones in love.''

The next five verses enrich our understanding of the depth of God's love for his people, in spite of their conviction in exile that he had forgotten all about them (v. 14). Two master images of intimacy are put forth. God can no more forget his people than a nursing mother can forget her child (v. 15). But even if a human mother might forget her child, the Lord could not possibly forget his.

A child in its mother's womb, a child at its mother's breast are eloquent examples of closeness. But the next image (v. 16b) is even more so. After a child is born and weaned, the child romps off. The lines etched on the palms of your hands are there to stay. Look at the palms of your own hands. An Islamic tradition says that the ninety-nine beautiful names of God are symbolically engraved there. Any carnival palmist will, for a fee, read your past and your future in those lines. The Lord's relationship with Israel is that close and that decisive and that indelible.

From v. 16b through v. 18, the poetic metaphors are more difficult to comprehend. They slip in and out of focus. What are those ''walls'' in v. 16b? Who is that gathering ''they'' of v. 18? In his Anchor Bible commentary, John L. McKenzie suggests an answer to the first question. Tattooed on the Lord's palms may be the blueprint of Jerusalem. The answer to the second question remains obscure, but they are surely builders and not destroyers. The latter are on the way out (v. 17b). The climactic picture repeats the joyful one of v. 13. Israel is at home, decked out in her jewels like a bride. People are streaming from far and near to do her honor. Lift up your eyes and see *that* future, O Israel. So take down your harps and sing the Lord's song even now, in your hostage situation.

SECOND LESSON: 1 CORINTHIANS 4:1–13

Paul still has the internecine quarrels in Corinth on his mind in this final reading from the 1 Corinthian sequence, as well as their evident criticisms of his own ministry.

The sarcasm in vv. 8–10 again plays on the theme of wisdom and foolishness. But it also adds further hints about the puffed-up state of mind among some of the church members. They seem to think that they have fully arrived in the kingdom, that they are already reigning monarchs with royal wealth. At this point in the letter one begins to wonder what kind of colorful details Chloe's people included in their report of what life was like in the church at Corinth (1:11).

In contrast, Paul gives us a catalogue of his own sufferings. He is fond of making lists. This one is not as extensive or as detailed as that in 2 Cor. 11:23–28, but it makes equally clear the fact that the life of a traveling evangelist in the first-century Mediterranean world was not an easy one. In v. 11 Paul ticks off five verbs to describe his condition. The translations necessarily lose the intensity of that sentence. He hungers, he thirsts, he shivers; he endures beatings and homelessness. Furthermore he is a manual laborer, working hard to support himself.

It is difficult to decide whether Paul is using the first person plural in a Queen Victoria fashion or whether he really intends to describe both his own condition and that of his fellow apostles as well. We need to keep reminding ourselves that Paul was always part of a team ministry.

The most striking aspect of this whole passage is the great chasm between 4:1 and 4:13. Paul and his companions should be regarded "as servants of Christ and stewards of the mysteries of God." Instead they are regarded as "the refuse of the world, the offscouring of all things." TEV makes the last two terms perhaps overly graphic when it renders v. 13, "We are no more than this world's garbage; we are the scum of the earth to this very hour!" Both Greek terms translated "refuse" and "offscouring" in the RSV may have cultic references and hence suggest something close to "scapegoats."

In any case, the present state of God's messengers in the eyes of the world is a far cry from the proper way to look upon them. They should be seen as Christ's "servants." The term once meant the rowers on the bottom deck of a galley. This nautical connotation has an intriguing (if fanciful) connection with the church under the figure of a ship. They should also be seen as "stewards." The *oikonomos* was the major-domo, the person in charge of someone else's household, a position of great trust. The "mysteries of God" for which these apostles are responsible are not in this context the sacraments, as some later Christian traditions came to understand the phrase, but rather the *kerygma,* the divine revelation they are entrusted to preach.

Given the renewed emphasis on a broader and deeper understanding of stewardship in today's churches, the idea of "stewards" in this passage might be the most interesting and relevant aspect to develop in your sermon.

GOSPEL: MATTHEW 6:24–34

Ours is an age of anxiety in a new key. Millions of human beings must still worry every day about what they will eat and how they will buy clothes for their children. But other millions, freed from worry about the basic necessities of life, find their anxiety fed daily by the evening network news. Threats of nuclear holocaust, global terrorism, environmental disaster give even our school-children nightmares. And all of us have anxiety about personal illness and our own death. You need to add any special anxieties that beset your own congregation. The Gospel today wheels all these faithless fears and not-so-foolish anxieties into surgery.

Matthew has structured this portion of his Gospel with artistic skill. The opening saying (v. 24) is a call for single-mindedness echoed in the next-to-last verse (v. 33) about seeking one thing above all else. Luke has used the same mammon saying in quite a different place in his Gospel, separated from the sayings on anxiety which he also found in Q.

It is curious that the RSV retained "mammon" in v. 24. The word is archaic in English even though it is a direct transliteration of the *mamōna* in the text. In an unusual bow to Scripture, my Webster's dictionary cites Matt. 6:24 in giving the probable etymology of the word. It defines it as riches, or wealth as an "evil, more or less deified." The TEV, JB and NEB have quite properly updated the word to "money." NEB has underlined the idolatry implied in the verse by putting a capital on Money. People who have two ultimate concerns are schizophrenic.

The "therefore" that introduces v. 25 thereby announced that a prescription for this mental illness will follow. It is as if a therapist were guiding us out of our money-grabbing fixation by turning our eyes away from the almighty dollar. We are, in fact, urged to look at the heavens and the earth—the same two dimensions of our space that Isaiah summoned to sing for joy in the first lesson today.

"Birds of the air" (v. 26) and "lilies of the field" (v. 28) have a

hallowed place in English literature. You might want to demyth-
ologize them, to make them homely for the ordinary bird-watchers
and gardeners in your congregation. Consider the robin. God feeds it
with worms. Robins don't need to stockpile them. Consider the dan-
delions. You are going to mow them down tomorrow morning but if
you look closely today you may discover that they are more beautiful
than the embroidered robes of the fabulous King Solomon, who
"excelled all the kings of the earth in riches" (1 Kings 10:23).

God knows that we need food and clothing. God provides it. Everything we have that sustains life is his largesse. Furthermore this
passage is persuasive testimony that he has filled the world with
beauty. Add cardinals, orioles, and great blue herons to the robin.
Add columbine, anemone, and chicory to the dandelion.

You need to be alerted to the blatant romanticism in these last two
paragraphs, however. Paul Minear remarked recently that birds and
grass are dubious proofs of God's care because they are so transient.
But so, I would add, are we.

The last two verses of this reading raise a problem, although you
may want to consider carefully what new meaning they give to the
passage. But v. 34 is an anticlimax. Matthew alone has it. Verse 34a is
a proverb independent of the preceding section, and v. 34b is another
popular axiom reinforcing the contrast between today and tomorrow.
The verse seems to deflect attention from the true crux of this section,
the importance of seeking first, foremost, and as top priority God's
kingdom. Making that an ultimate concern is synonymous with seeking his righteousness. When one does, we are told, our anxious
tensions may relax.

To return to earlier metaphors, I doubt whether today's gospel
surgery can remove all of our anxieties. But it may well help toward a
biopsy report that they are not malignant. Or again, I doubt whether
an injunction to seek one thing first will cure my schizophrenia, but I
know that looking around me helps.

The Transfiguration of Our Lord
The Last Sunday After the Epiphany

Lutheran	Roman Catholic	Episcopal	Pres/UCC/Chr	Meth/COCU
Exod. 24:12, 15–18	Dan. 7:9–10, 13–14	Exod. 24:12 (13–14), 15–18	Ezek. 34:11–17	Exod. 24:12–18
2 Pet. 1:16–19 (20–21)	2 Pet. 1:16–19	Phil. 3:7–14	1 Cor. 15:20–28	2 Pet. 1:16–21
Matt. 17:1–9	Matt. 17:1–9	Matt. 17:1–9	Matt. 25:31–46	Matt. 17:1–9

Today's three readings are intimately interconnected. Together they round off the Epiphany season with another great manifestation of the Lord's anointed, yet one with reverberating echoes from the season's first Sunday when we remembered Jesus' baptism. Together they also prepare us for the forty days of Lent which are almost upon us—and point beyond to the Easter epiphany of the Risen Lord. On this transitional day, we are invited to climb mountains.

FIRST LESSON: EXODUS 24:12, 15–18

Topography and chronology are both important in coming to terms with this section of Exodus. The geographical setting is Mount Sinai, the traditional name which is synonymous with Mount Horeb, "the mountain of God" (cf. Exod. 3:1). It would be helpful, especially if you live in flat country, to study in a good Bible atlas a photograph of Jebel Musa, the mountain tradition identifies as *the* mountain. The scenery is rugged in the extreme. Going up that rocky peak which rises to 7,457 feet must have been more like climbing the Grand Teton than like a day's hike in the Berkshires.

Three references to time occur in this passage. All are significant. In v. 16 we are told that the cloud covered the mountain for six days, but that the Lord spoke out of it on the seventh. The symbolism of the Sabbath is almost too obvious to deserve comment. When does the Lord speak to us most surely?

In v. 18b we are told that Moses was on the mountain forty days and forty nights. Forty was also a symbolic figure in ancient Israel and it remains so in Jewish-Christian thought today. Israel was in the wilderness for forty years, for which read a long time. Jesus was in the wilderness for forty days and forty nights, the same length of time that Moses spent on Sinai. We are about to enter a church season of forty days, although it can only be so counted by a bit of ecclesiastical legerdemain. The idea of forty as a long time may be related to the fact that it is longer than a lunar month; but whatever its origin, it here tells us that Moses spent many a night up on Sinai.

The Lord's direction to Moses in v. 12 offers a superb text for a whole sermon: "Come up to me . . . and wait." The words evoke Samuel Beckett's existentialist play, *Waiting for Godot.* In contrast to the emptiness of that waiting, however, the Lord makes a promise which he keeps. Moses does not wait in vain. "To wait upon the Lord" has acquired rich meanings in Jewish and Christian history.

Verses 15–18 betray different documentary origins. Poor Moses seems in fact to climb the mountain twice in these verses. The final redaction of the Book of Exodus retains a number of doublets. But this passage should be seen as a deliberately chosen way to conclude the great section on the covenant which begins in 19:1 when the Israelites first arrived at the mountain and the Lord first spoke to Moses out of the mountain (19:3). In the frame between 19:1 and 24:18 come the sealing of Israel's covenant relationship with the Lord, the giving of the Decalogue, and the Book of the Covenant (20:22—23:19), Israel's very ancient law code. The whole section, therefore, presents the heart of Israel's historical faith.

For this reason, what the Lord says in 24:12 should be read in the light of what he said in 19:4, with its lyrical expression of close covenant relationship: "You have seen what I did to the Egyptians, and how I bore you on eagles' wings and brought you to myself." That gracious act precedes the giving of stone tables of commandment.

Again in this reading we have the great symbols of God's presence, cloud and fire, which we met earlier in Epiphany. These symbols in this context do not permit rationalistic speculation about literal volcanic action on Mount Sinai. The metaphors of mountain storms make possible powerful religious poetry. One should compare 24:17 with Ps. 18:1–19 and Psalm 29, for example, as they "ascribe to the Lord glory and strength" and summon us to worship.

SECOND LESSON: 2 PETER 1:16–19 (20–21)

We are back on the holy mountain, this time in the company of

Peter, eyewitness to the transfiguration of Jesus and direct auditor of the divine voice.

Most scholars think this epistle is one of the latest NT writings, one which comes from the subapostolic age. Among the reasons for this dating are its close literary dependence on Jude, its reference to the Pauline letters as Scripture (3:16), the kind of false teaching that is attacked, and the concern expressed over the delay of the Parousia. The writing would thus be pseudonymous, attributed to Peter to support its authority. None of this would rule out the possibility of genuine Petrine reminiscence, however, handed down in the oral tradition of the church.

The author is intent on contrasting the testimony of eyewitnesses with the "cleverly devised myths" (1:16) of those who are bringing "destructive heresies" (2:1) into the community. The literal translation "myths" is preferable to the paraphrase "made-up legends" (TEV), because the allusion is to the kind of cosmic mythology that was the stock in trade of the early gnostics. They were not primarily interested in human historical events, alleged or otherwise.

Eyewitness status is the hallmark, on the other hand, of the true apostles. They knew themselves to be witnesses of the Resurrection; they were those who had seen the Lord (cf. Luke 1:2; Acts 1:22; 1 Cor. 15:3–11). Here the author claims that he saw the "majesty" of the Lord Jesus Christ. The same word is used of God (Luke 9:43) and of Artemis, the great goddess of the Ephesians (Acts 19:27), although in the latter case it is translated as "magnificence." Since 2 Peter opens with a rare NT identification of Jesus Christ as God (v. 1:1; RSV margin), full divine majesty is surely implied in 1:16.

In the next two verses the author retells the story of what happened on the Mount of Transfiguration. It lacks the rich detail of the synoptic accounts, as we shall see; but it is patently the same event. The author assumes that his readers already know the story of that epiphany of the Lord, that manifestation of his true identity. The words borne to Jesus by "the Majestic Glory" are those we hear again shortly from Matthew. Peter heard them on the spot.

The authority and proper interpretation of Scripture are next ranked alongside eyewitness testimony as offering protection for the community from false teaching. Verses 19–21 raise a number of problems of understanding, however. Since the lectionary offers the options of omitting vv. 20–21, I would certainly do so. This evades some of the obscurity of the last long sentence. More positively, it leaves the listener with two splendid images of light more fitting for the transfiguration than questions of scriptural hermeneutics. Artistically, liturgically, it is best to end the reading with anticipation ringing in our ears: "Until the day dawns and the morning star rises in your hearts" (v. 19b).

This decision does not avoid all the problems in the text. If I read v. 19a in a student paper, I would immediately ask in the margin, "More sure" than what? The text does not say. Commentators disagree as to the comparison intended. The most satisfying suggestion is that no comparison is intended, that the sense is simply that the prophetic word is "*very* sure." By "prophetic word" here is probably meant Scripture in general. That is the lamp now "shining in a dark place." We are to pay attention to its light for the time being.

But the Day will dawn (v. 19b). This is a sure and certain hope, and it refers to the Day of the Lord. The author signaled that in v. 16 when he spoke of "the power and coming" of Christ. Here he equates that Day with the rising of the morning star in people's hearts. It is not necessary to interpret this as subjective individual experience, as some commentators do. One function of morning stars is to sing together, to cause people collectively to shout for joy (cf. Job. 38:7).

When 2 Peter was written, the morning star was already a metaphor for Jesus Christ in Christian vocabulary. In Rev. 22:16 Jesus is called "the bright morning star." The morning star is promised in Rev. 2:28 to those who hold fast until Christ comes. Within the "great code" of Scripture, to borrow Northrop Frye's fine phrase, 2 Peter's use of the term evokes both OT and NT images.

Within that same great code there is also another echo here. Any astronomer's almanac can tell you about the morning star in any particular season. It is that star, usually the planet Venus, which is visible in the eastern sky just before sunrise. Our Epiphany season began with a star appearing in the east. The star moved ahead of the Magi and came to rest over the place where the young child lay.

GOSPEL: MATTHEW 17:1–9

Matthew's account of the transfiguration is fuller than that of the author of 2 Peter. It also differs from those of Mark and Luke in several important details. Because the voice from heaven uses the same words in 2 Peter and Matthew, one guesses that Matthew was the synoptic version the Petrine writer assumed his readers knew already.

The voice says slightly different things in Mark and Luke, although with some textual variants in each case. All three, however, add the imperative, "Listen to him." This is a new note, not found explicitly in 2 Peter or even implicitly in the baptismal story where, a few weeks ago, we heard virtually the same words that are repeated here in Matt. 17:5 (cf. 3:17).

Matthew nuances his Markan source in four other distinctive ways. Both he and Luke reverse the order of Elijah and Moses as Jesus' conversational companions. After all, Moses is prior to Elijah in time. But only Matthew tells us that Jesus' face "shone like the sun" (v. 2). Only Matthew says his garments "became white as light" (v. 2). Only Matthew qualifies the overshadowing cloud as "bright" (v. 5). Such intensification of the dazzling quality of this experience must surely be deliberate redaction on the part of the evangelist.

The fourth noteworthy difference between Matthew and the other Synoptics is more than a detail. Matthew alone adds the moving interchange between Jesus and his disciples in vv. 6–7. Overawed by what they have seen, Peter, James, and John prostrate themselves. But Jesus comes and touches them. This is not some stranger who has overwhelmed them. This is the same man they have been talking with, eating with, walking with for many weeks. Now he reaches out his hand to them and reassures them once again, "Have no fear" (v. 7).

Peter's offer to build three booths (v. 4) needs to be clarified for your congregation. This offer is common to all the Synoptics, although only Matthew's Peter is deferential enough to add that he will do so only if Jesus wants him to. The "booths" would be similar to those Jews build for the joyous feast of Tabernacles or Succoth, originally an agricultural festival celebrating the fall harvest. By Matthew's time the festival had also been historicized, linked with the sojourning life of the Israelites after the exodus. Here the booths or tents therefore bear both the connotation of joy and that of commemorating a historical event.

Most evident in this reading, almost needing no comment, are the typological references back to the Exodus passage that was our first reading. Both include the time references to six days. Another Sabbath has rolled around in Matt. 17:1, another Lord's Day set aside for worship. Another cloud sits down upon the holy mountain. A voice again comes from the cloud. In all three of the Synoptics these typological references are intentional and decisive. The manifestation of the glory of the Lord on Mount Sinai was a manifestation of the same glory that dazzled Peter and James and John on this mountain this morning.

Preaching about the transfiguration, even given this magnificent set of lections, is risky business. You can easily stress the revelation of Christ's identity to the point that you lose contact in the cloud on that mountain with Peter and the rest of your congregation. Or you can err in the other direction and reduce the enormity of that reported explosion of brilliant light to the power of a sixty-watt bulb.

If that were the only choice, I would opt for the lower wattage. In my opinion the danger in our churches of making Jesus less than human far exceeds the danger of making him less than God. But Matthew has helped us get beyond an either/or choice of this sort. The key here, in my judgment, is in v. 8b, "they saw no one but Jesus only." This means, of course, that Moses and Elijah had disappeared. But it makes a far more important theological point. It removes the shining cloud and the Moses-like countenance and the incandescent robes. It leaves us looking at "Jesus only."

Occasionally in our lives some of us have had profound spiritual experiences which tilt the mundane universe for us, which transfigure it for us, which help us to see everything with new eyes. Such experiences do not last but they leave us changed. So it was, I think, with the disciples who witnessed the transfiguration. For a few moments they saw the whole world charged with God's grandeur. The grandeur faded, but Jesus did not leave them.

Ending the reading with v. 9 is again an anticlimax, although it serves the function of pulling our thoughts ahead to Easter. Many responsible interpreters think that the whole account we have just heard is, in fact, a displaced Resurrection appearance. Be that as it may, we are thinking about it at the end of Epiphany. In the service of this season, the Gospel tells us to look at Jesus and listen to him. When we do, we see the one who is the Light of the world and hear him sending us on mission to all people far and near.